ZOMBRE

AN UNDEAD ANTHOLOGY

Zombre
A Borderline Press Undead Anthology

First published: November 2013

10 9 8 7 6 5 4 3 2 1

ISBN: 978-0-9926972-2-8

Borderline Press
45 Fullingdale Road
Northampton
NN3 2PZ

www.borderline-press.com

Editor - Will Vigar

Printed by Berforts Ltd

DEADICATION

Dedicating a book of Zombie stories to anyone as a mark of affection and thanks seems something of a peculiar thing to do. "Thank you so much! Here's a bunch of corpses". See what I mean?

That said, without the love and support of Andy Malinowski, Phil Hall, Sunny Jim, Ramzi Musa, Rachel Barlow, Ross Walker and The Eternal Wayne Moores, this dedication wouldn't have needed to be written.

Nothing says 'I love you' more than a bunch of walking corpses.

CONTENTS

Long Overdue by Phil Buckenham

Lunchtime by Peter Clack

Family Man by Baden James Mellonie & Richard Whitaker

So, This One Day in Judea by Nigel Lowrey

Zennui by Milōs Kûntz

Nursapocalypse by Mitz

Zeddlers by Si Spencer & Ash Fielder

Belonging by Kim Winter

Covers by Tom Box Frontispieces by Sarah Hardy

Pinups by Ramzi Musa, Kelvin Green, Phil Buckenham

Photography by P.M. Hall Additional design by Will Vigar

Additional lettering by July Stapleton & Ande Morgenson

Typeface: Tom's New Roman

available from Divide By Zero - http://fonts.tom7.com

Zombre is the first Borderline Press Anthology (BPA001)

Undead Letter Office

The first horror movie I was ever allowed to watch was Plague of the Zombies; a Hammer Horror that, even then, was of dubious quality. I was probably about 8 and it was part of a season of movies on ITV that also featured Vincent Price in both The Fly and The Abominable Dr Phibes. I became something of a Horror Hound and would smuggle Horror magazines into my room and away from my parents' disapproving gaze. I saved my pocket money up to buy the Aurora Horror dioramas and hid them in a box, the luminous body parts casting a baleful light under my bed.

The only horror movies I was uncomfortable with were the new breed of Zombie Movies. Whereas movies like Karloff's White Zombie and Hammer's Plague of the Zombies had a certain quaintness to them, and crucially, I think, had a basis in the Haitian voodoo practices, Romero's Zombies, and those of that ilk were cruel, unthinking and ravenous.

Where I could believe and be comforted by the notion of a person in a trance-like-state doing someone's evil bidding, and could feel some sympathy with them, I couldn't feel anything for the zombies in Romero's take. I enjoyed the movies, but it was a world away from Der Golem and Cesar in Das Cabinet de Dr Caligari; there was no humanity to hold onto or to identify with. One of the things I loved most about horror movies is that they are essentially morality tales. You often identified with the alienation felt by the 'monsters'. Didn't you feel sorry for Frankenstein's creation? I bet you did.

But you can't feel that for Zombies. Once they rise, that's pretty much it. You know where the story is going. I watched the movies, enjoyed them but, for me, the genre got increasingly thin. It became more about gimmicks or gore and less about coherent stories.

Then, on one dull summer's day, I went to the cinema and saw World War Z. It was okay, but somewhere buried in the dazzling CGI fest, there was something much more quiet, more intimate. It was a thread that was unresolved; almost as if the studio had uttered the cliché, "horror fans don't want plot, they want action!" and edited out anything that made any of the characters believable.

I wondered what Max Brooks' original book was like. I read it and it blew me away. It wasn't about zombies eating brains; it was about peoples reactions to a zombie apocalypse, remembrances of the cataclysm and the appalling mistakes made by governments, the army, officials and just ordinary people. This is exactly what I wanted from my zombie stories: humanity.

When I was asked to put this book together, the brief I was given was simple. "Do a Zombie Anthology". I decided I didn't want lumbering idiots having their brains blown out and put out a strict "No Romero Homages, No Walking Dead homages and no Shaun of the Dead homages." I wanted the contributors to do something different; something small, something intimate; something thought provoking, satirical or bat-shit crazy.

And we have all of those. And more.

In putting this anthology together, I've been privileged to discover the first ever zombie, the last act of a desperate man, blasphemy, comedy, satire, pathos, the surreal and Nazi Zombies on Mars.

Even I didn't see that one coming. Will Vigar October 2013

Lurch

The day they said
death was no longer the final stage
was the day we all died

Bodies bother us
because the politics of death is intimate
it is ours to own

Termination is personal
it affects all but not in the same way
the dead don't grieve

There is no exquisite corpse
just biodegradable materials
the fertiliser of the gods

When the dead rise
the disgust is palpable
the ultimate body horror

Why do they eat brains?
Why do they not cry for themselves?
And why do they lurch?

SOMEWHERE IN THE COLLECTIVE CONSCIOUSNESS
ONCE IN A TIME OF SUPERSTITION AND FEAR - MAN'S IMAGINATION GAVE WAY TO THE TERRORS OF THE UNKNOWN...
BATTENBURG
A TALE OF THE UNDEAD KING

BUT AS MAN GREW LESS AFRAID - SO HIS TERRORS WERE FORCED TO ADAPT.
UNTIL A DAY WOULD COME -
WHEN THEY WOULD HAVE NO OPTION -
BUT TO TAKE BACK THE FEAR -
THAT THEY HAD LOST.

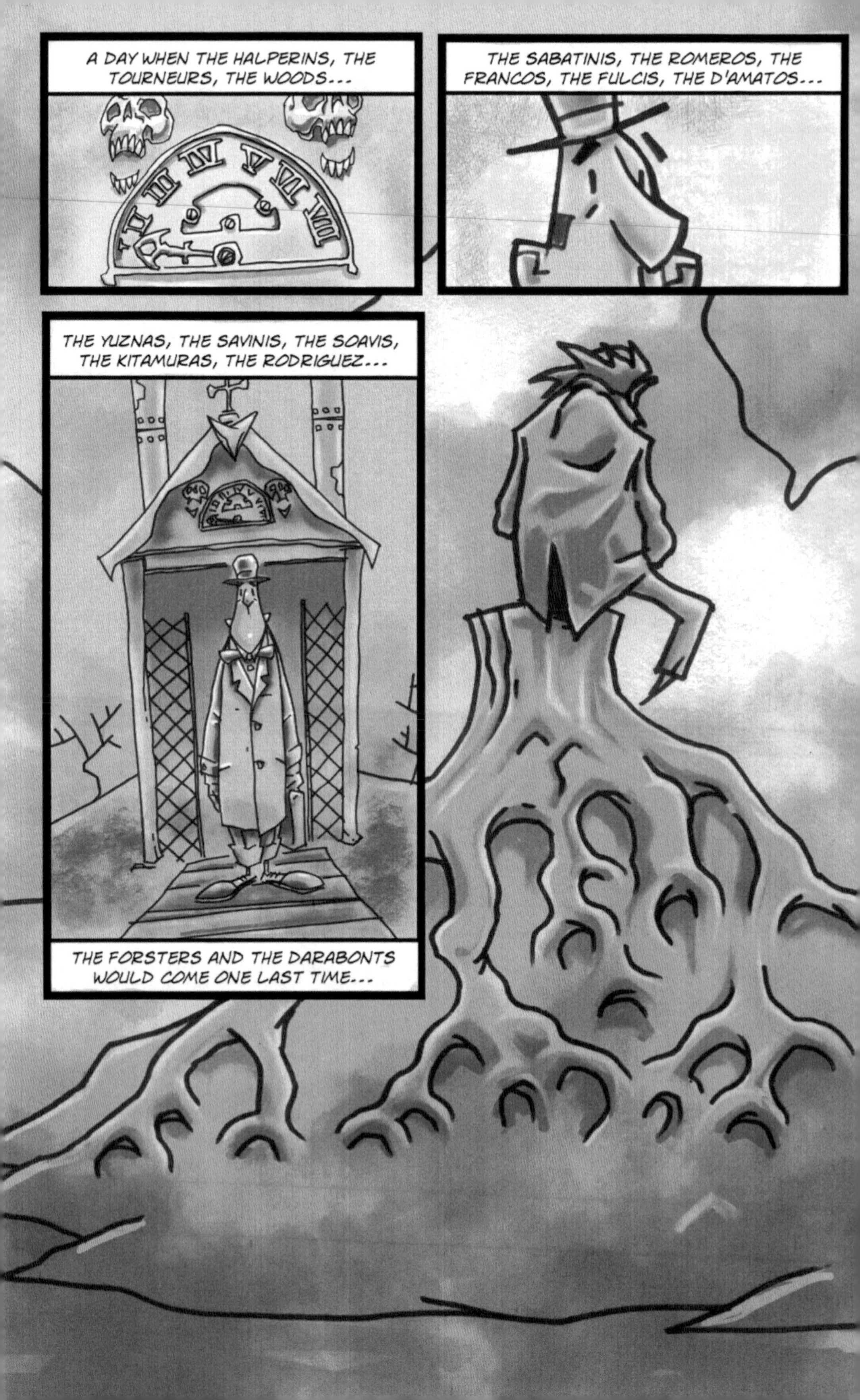
A DAY WHEN THE HALPERINS, THE TOURNEURS, THE WOODS...
THE SABATINIS, THE ROMEROS, THE FRANCOS, THE FULCIS, THE D'AMATOS...
THE YUZNAS, THE SAVINIS, THE SOAVIS, THE KITAMURAS, THE RODRIGUEZ...
THE FORSTERS AND THE DARABONTS WOULD COME ONE LAST TIME...

AND THE TERROR WOULD SCREAM INTO THE FACE OF MAN... ENOUGH!!!
AHEM! MR NZAMBI?
I WAS A GOD - ONCE.
YES.
AH GOOD!.. MY NAME IS CARROON... VICTOR CARROON.
OF THE PRAGUE KAFKANULAR FILM CORPORATION!
SCRIPT DEPARTMENT.
ERM... RECENTLY WE RECIEVED THE FINAL DRAFT OF A FILM SCRIPT...
WHICH WE FEEL THAT YOU AS LICENSOR AND ORIGINAL ZOMBIE MAY BE INTERESTED IN SANCTIONING...
THE MONETARY RETURNS ARE POTENTIALLY HUGE...

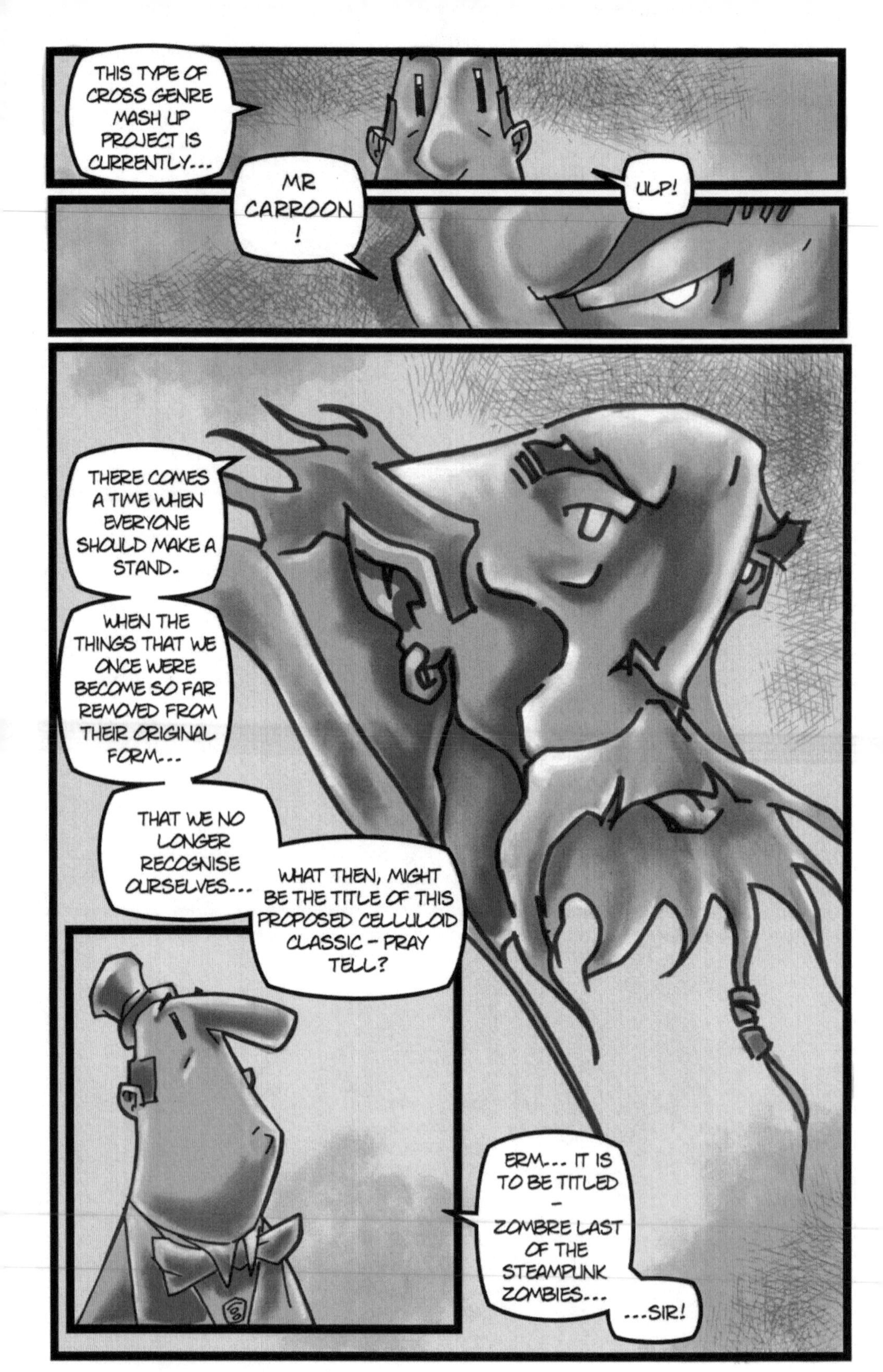
THIS TYPE OF CROSS GENRE MASH UP PROJECT IS CURRENTLY...
MR CARROON !
ULP!
THERE COMES A TIME WHEN EVERYONE SHOULD MAKE A STAND.
WHEN THE THINGS THAT WE ONCE WERE BECOME SO FAR REMOVED FROM THEIR ORIGINAL FORM...
THAT WE NO LONGER RECOGNISE OURSELVES...
WHAT THEN, MIGHT BE THE TITLE OF THIS PROPOSED CELLULOID CLASSIC - PRAY TELL?
ERM... IT IS TO BE TITLED - ZOMBRE LAST OF THE STEAMPUNK ZOMBIES...
...SIR!

REALLY!!
URM - YES!?
CATCHY!
LETS TALK ROYALTY RATES MR CARROON!
BATTENBURG?!
ONE DAY PERHAPS... BUT NOT TODAY!!!

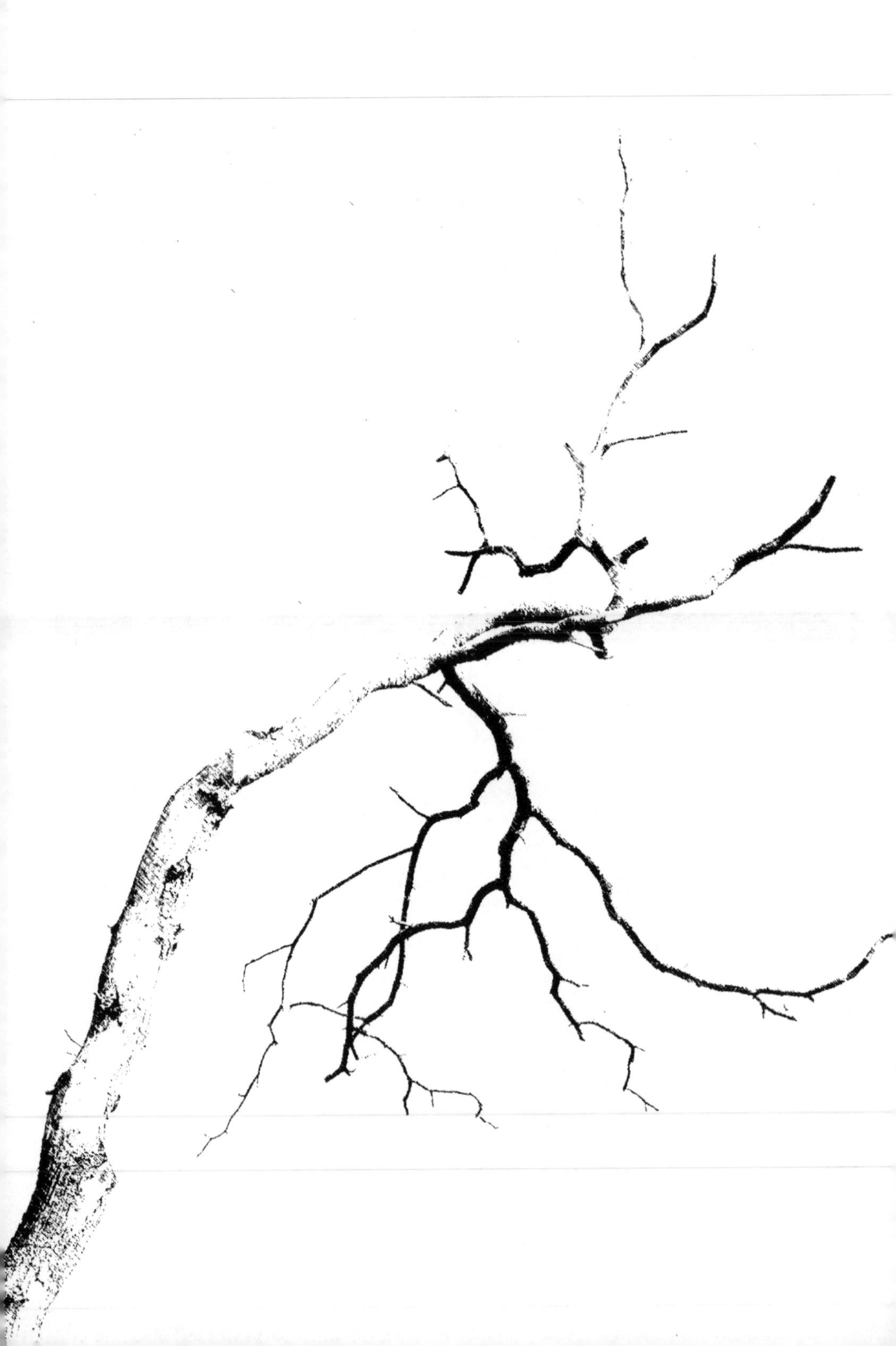

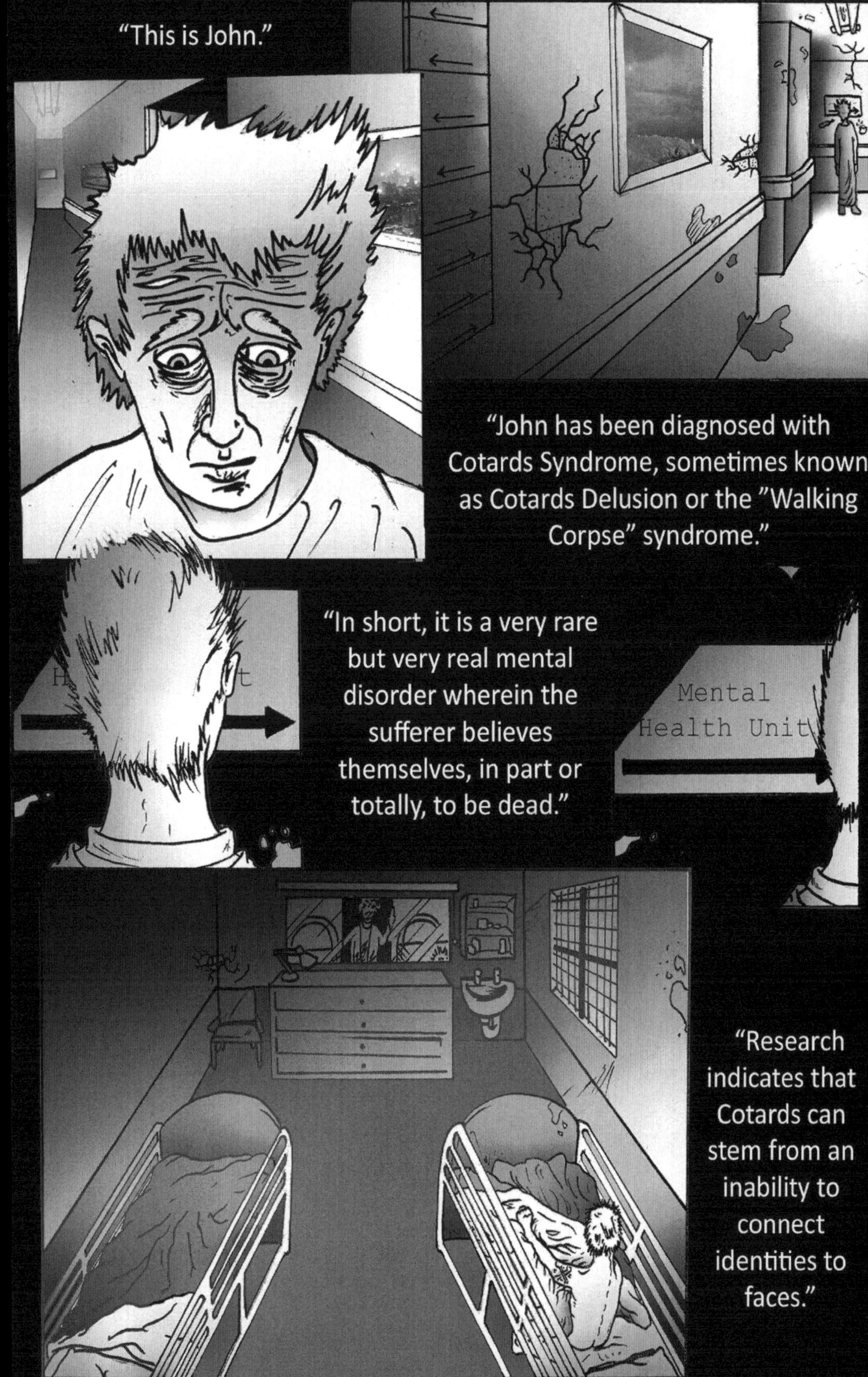
"This is John."
"John has been diagnosed with Cotards Syndrome, sometimes known as Cotards Delusion or the "Walking Corpse" syndrome."
"In short, it is a very rare but very real mental disorder wherein the sufferer believes themselves, in part or totally, to be dead."
Mental
Health Unit
"Research indicates that Cotards can stem from an inability to connect identities to faces."

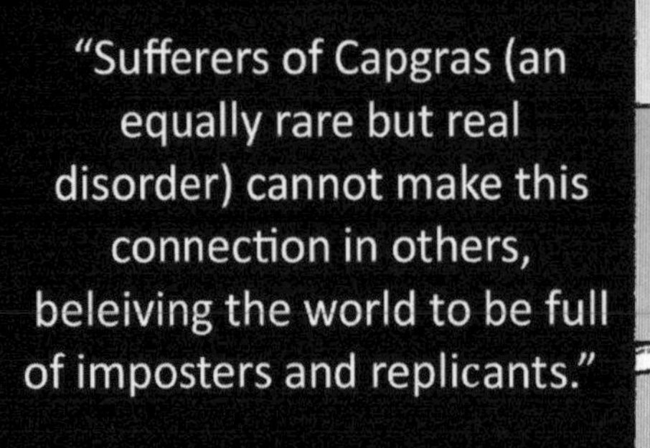

"Sufferers of Capgras (an equally rare but real disorder) cannot make this connection in others, beleiving the world to be full of imposters and replicants."

"Cotard sufferers on the other hand, fail to make this connection internally, and thus don't recognise their own continued existance."

"Additionally, the syndrome is sometimes physically identified by lesions in the Parietal Lobe."

THE IMPORTANCE OF CORRECTLY IDENTIFYING THE UNDEAD.

Script by Richard Worth / Art by James Oliver Firkins

"One day, as John was leaving his dead end and utterly disapointing job for his cosier, more intimate flat - as the estate agent had generously misrepresented it..."

"He was attacked by a mob of beastly youths"

"'What kind of monsters could do this?' exclaimed Marjorie Venkman, the elderly woman who found the unconscious and bloodied John sometime later."

"John was rushed to hospital and an attempt was made to reach his emergency contact; Stephanie Frost."

"Stephanie, the woman who jilted John at the alter, was unreachable. She was on holiday with her new lover and John's former workmate, David, in Mexico."

"A major symptom of Cotards is depression and the withdrawal from others; However John's various allergies and ailments mean he is unable to undergo a traditional pharmaceutical treatment."

"In it's place John has been asked to join group therapy. This has been largely ineffective save for one interaction."

"Fellow patient, Jeremy (advanced paranoia) simply pointed out that dead people don't have a pulse and that John must be up to something."

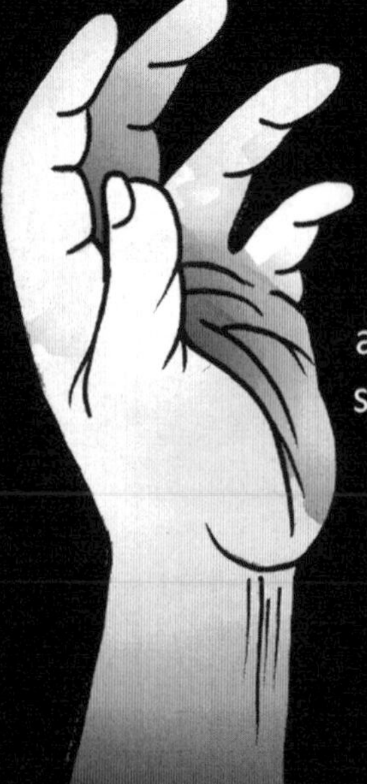

"in fantastically rare accounts, some Cotard sufferers have beleived themselves to be immortal... ...John has become obsessed with his pulse..."

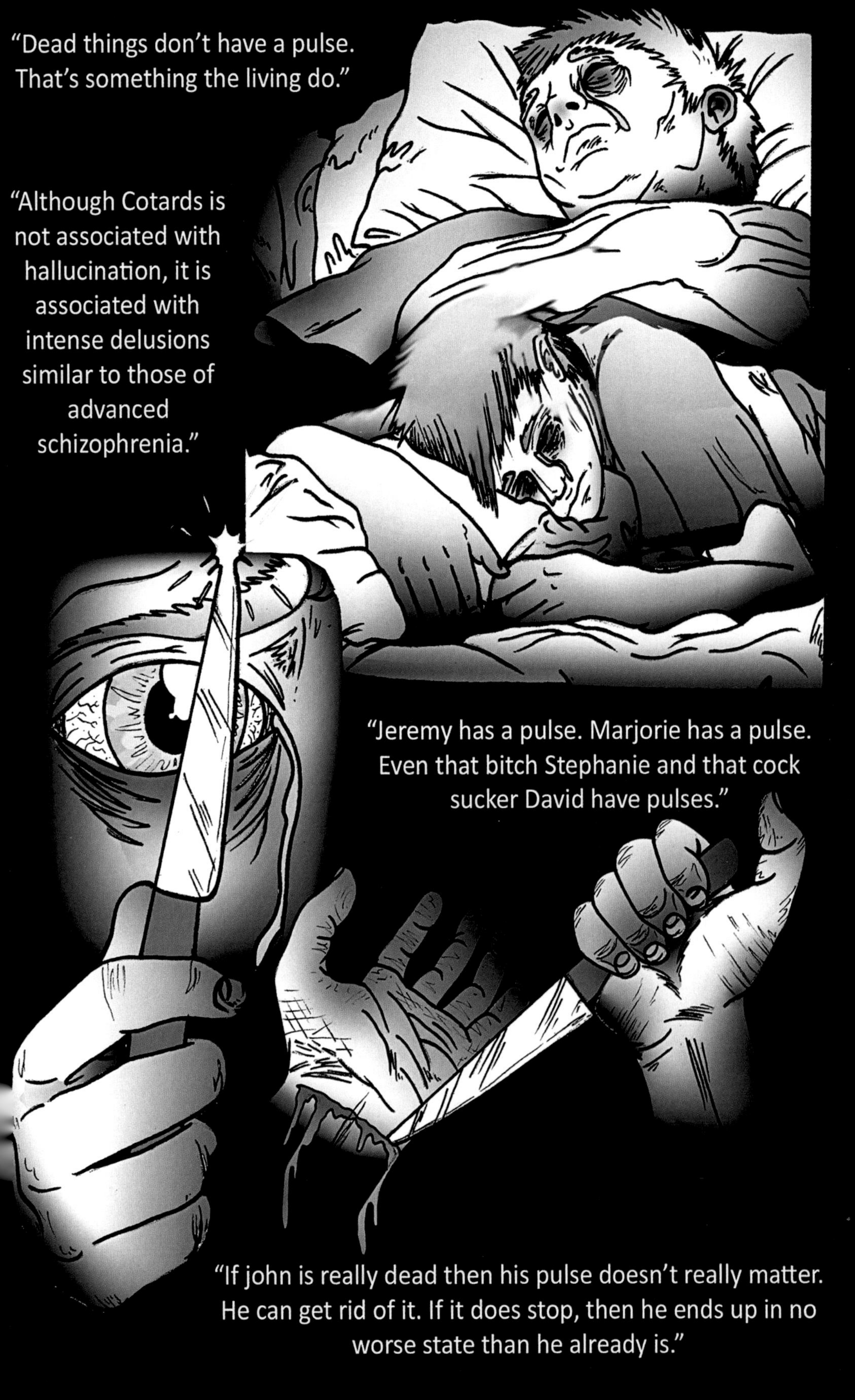
"Dead things don't have a pulse. That's something the living do."
"Although Cotards is not associated with hallucination, it is associated with intense delusions similar to those of advanced schizophrenia."
"Jeremy has a pulse. Marjorie has a pulse. Even that bitch Stephanie and that cock sucker David have pulses."
"If john is really dead then his pulse doesn't really matter. He can get rid of it. If it does stop, then he ends up in no worse state than he already is."

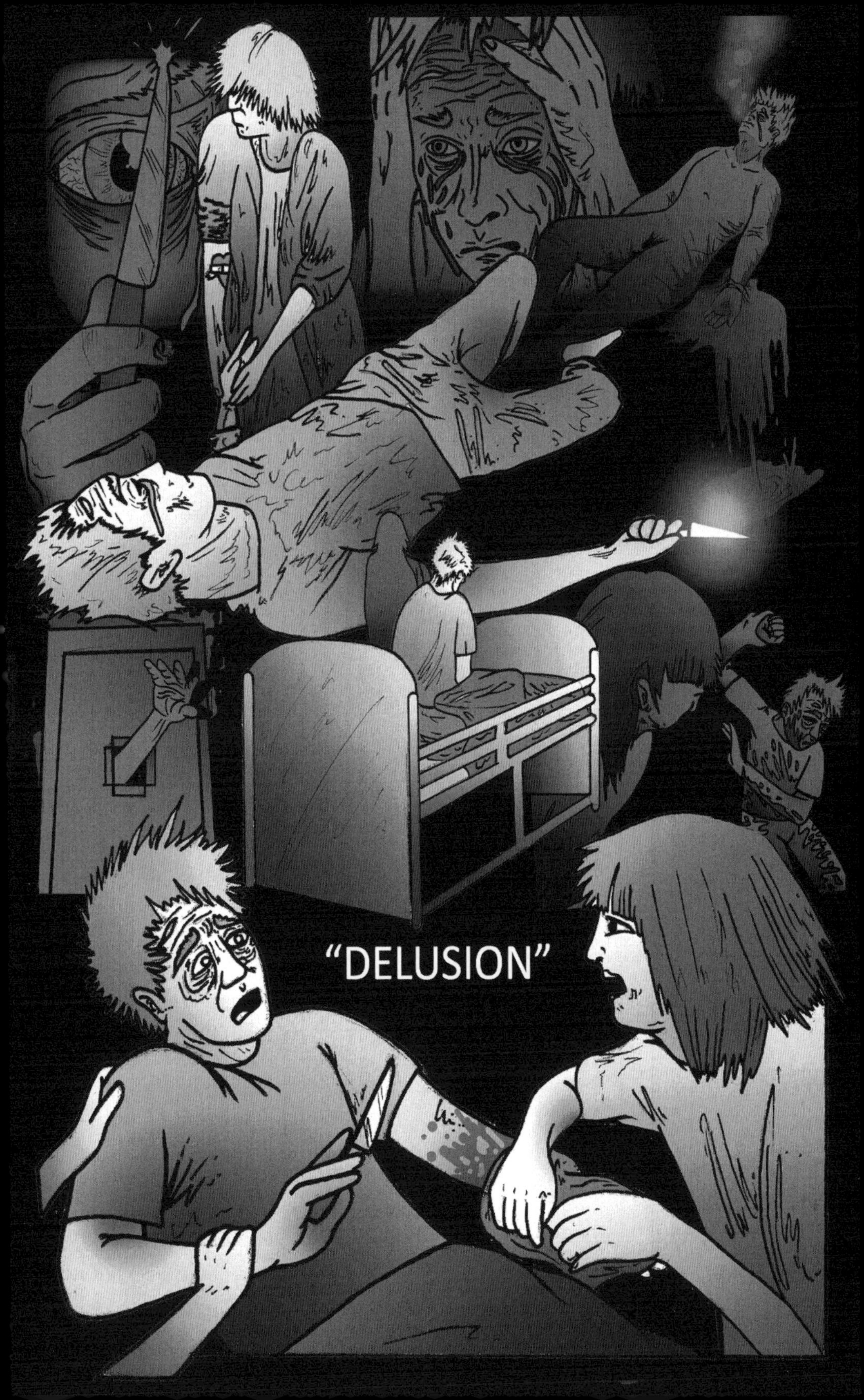
"DELUSION"

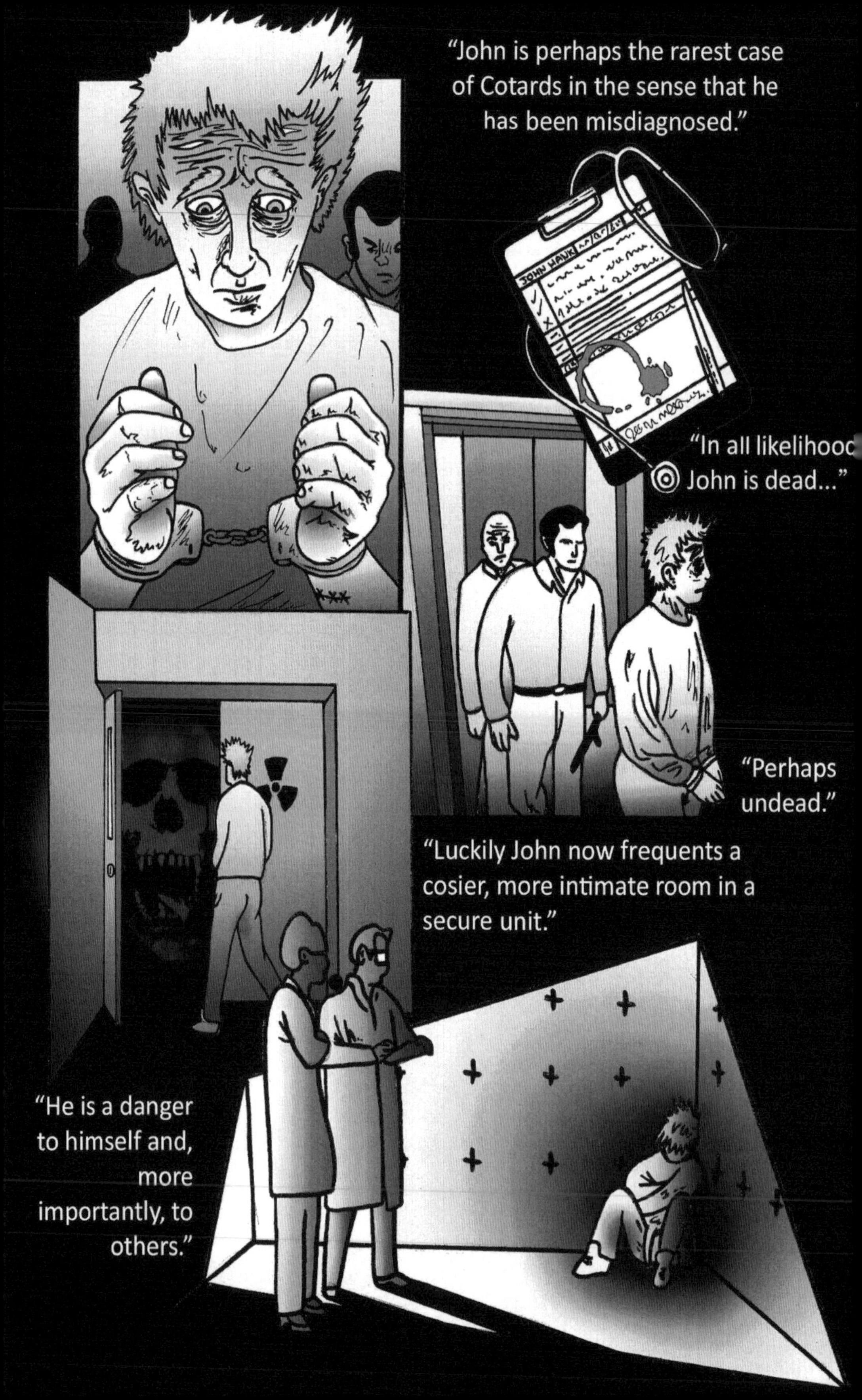

“John is perhaps the rarest case of Cotards in the sense that he has been misdiagnosed.”
“In all likelihoo John is dead...”
“Perhaps undead.”
“Luckily John now frequents a cosier, more intimate room in a secure unit.”
“He is a danger to himself and, more importantly, to others.”

IMAGINARY KINGDOM

WRITER: JAY EALES
ARTIST: KRZYSZTOF OSTROWSKI

I'M NOT SURE WHAT TIPPED ME OFF THAT I'D GONE TONTO. WAS IT THAT I WAS SEEING THE WALKING DEAD EVERYWHERE? FOLKS DROPPING LIKE FLIES AND GETTING UP WITH A TASTE FOR MORE THAN KETCHUP?

BE MY FRIEND?
MAYBE IT WAS WHEN I STARTED HEARING VOICES IN MY HEAD.

WHEN I WAS A KID, I HAD THIS FRIEND, BILLYBONES. BEST MATE A GROWING BOY COULD HAVE. WE DID EVERYTHING TOGETHER.

HE STAYED WITH ME WHEN I FELL OUT OF THE TREE IN WOODY'S ORCHARD. HE GOT ME TO CLIMB THE BLOODY THING IN THE FIRST PLACE, MIND...

HE SHOWED ME HOW TO TURN STICKS INTO CATAPULTS, BOOMERANGS - ALL KINDS OF WEAPONS. ONLY THING WAS, NOBODY ELSE COULD SEE HIM BUT ME.

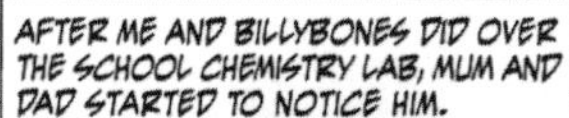

AFTER ME AND BILLYBONES DID OVER THE SCHOOL CHEMISTRY LAB, MUM AND DAD STARTED TO NOTICE HIM.

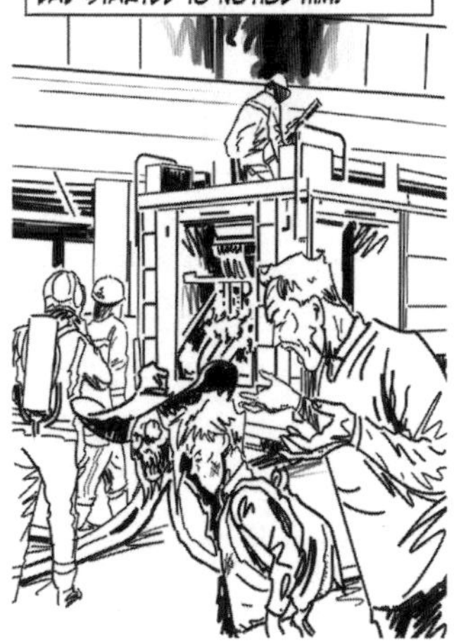

SENT ME TO ALL KINDS OF HEAD-SHRINKERS. DIDN'T UNDERSTAND MUCH OF WHAT THEY SAID, BUT OLD BILLYBONES, HE DIDN'T LIKE IT.

I HAD TO CHANGE SCHOOLS, AND ALONG WITH ALL MY OTHER FRIENDS, BILLYBONES QUIETLY WENT AWAY TOO. I HADN'T GIVEN HIM A THOUGHT IN YEARS. THEN, THE BIG WTF HAPPENED.

I CALL IT THE WTF BECAUSE NOBODY REALLY FIGURED OUT WHAT THE FUCK HAPPENED.

ONE DAY, EVERYONE'S WATCHING I'M A NONENTITY, GET ME OUT OF HERE, AND EATING POT NOODLES.

THE NEXT, PEOPLE START TO GET SICK. I MEAN, REALLY SICK.

IT TOOK DAYS BEFORE ANYONE TOOK IT SERIOUSLY. IT WAS WHEN THAT NEWSREADER BROUGHT UP A KIDNEY OVER THE CAMERA ON BREAKFAST TELLY, THAT PEOPLE SHAT THEMSELVES. TOO LATE, BY THEN.

THE GOVERNMENT FELL APART IMMEDIATELY, OF COURSE. WE'RE ALL IN THIS TOGETHER, THEY SAID AS THEY GOT ON THE PLANE.

I LIKE TO IMAGINE THEM CRACKING OPEN THE CHAMPERS, CONGRATULATING THEMSELVES FOR GIVING THE COUNTRY ONE FINAL SHAFT. THEN KEN CLARKE VAMPS OUT...

...AND THE 757 BECOMES JUST ANOTHER TIN OF CANNED FOOD.

FAST FORWARD A FEW MONTHS AND IT'S ALL GONE TO SHIT. EVERYONE OUT FOR THEMSELVES, AND WILLING TO KILL FOR THE LAST TIN OF TUNA.

YOU'D THINK WITH ALL THOSE ZOMBIE FILMS, THERE'D BE PEOPLE BANDING TOGETHER TO HOLD OFF THE RAVENING HORDES, BUT IT JUST ISN'T LIKE THAT.

WHAT WAS IT THATCHER SAID ABOUT THERE BEING NO SUCH THING AS SOCIETY? WELL, WELCOME TO YOUR WORLD, MAGGIE.
1925 -

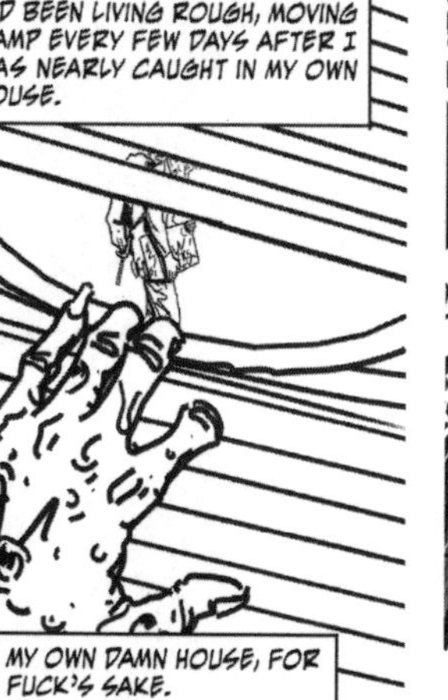
I'D BEEN LIVING ROUGH, MOVING CAMP EVERY FEW DAYS AFTER I WAS NEARLY CAUGHT IN MY OWN HOUSE.
MY OWN DAMN HOUSE, FOR FUCK'S SAKE.

I GOT COCKY. THIS GUY GRANT, WHO WAS PRETTY TASTY WITH A CRICKET BAT, SEEMED TO BE A STAND-UP INDIVIDUAL. WE'D STOOD AND BROKEN HEADS TOGETHER.

I LET SLIP ABOUT MY STASH OF BEEF JERKY STICKS, GRABBED BEFORE THE SUPERMARKET GOT TOO HAIRY WITH ZOMS AND HAD TO TORCH IT. SCHOOL ALL OVER AGAIN.

EARNED MYSELF A CRACKED SKULL FOR MY MISPLACED TRUST, BUT GOT A VALUABLE LESSON OUT OF IT.

TRUST NO FUCKER.

YOU WANT MY CANS?
COME GET SOME. I'VE GOT A 9 IRON WAITING FOR YOU, AND I'VE BEEN WORKING ON MY HANDICAP.

I'D NOT SPOKEN TO A LIVING SOUL FOR OVER TWO MONTHS WHEN BILLYBONES CAME CALLING FOR A SCHOOL REUNION.

FREAKED ME RIGHT OUT HE DID, SINCE I WAS SITTING ON A ROOF, WATCHING A STRAY SHAMBLER SWAYING AIMLESSLY IN MY DIRECTION.

I CALLED HIM DODGER ON ACCOUNT OF HIS CLOTHES BEING ALL 'JAMMY', WHEN BB PIPES UP, CLEAR AS A BELL.
HEY!
WATCH OUT!
THOUGHT FOR A MINUTE THAT DODGER WAS REPLYING TO ME. GOOD JOB I WASN'T PERCHED ON A SLOPE, OR I'D HAVE PITCHED OFF THE FRONT INTO THE STREET, LIKE MANNA FROM HEAVEN FOR THE DODGER.

BEHIND YOU!
AS IT WAS, BILLYBONES WAS TIPPING ME OFF ABOUT THE CRAWLING ZOM I HADN'T SPOTTED BEHIND ME.

AFTER THAT, THINGS SEEMED BETTER AGAIN.

BEN AND BILLYBONES, THE TEAM SUPREME.

WITH BB WATCHING MY BACK, I COULD TAKE A FEW MORE CHANCES. HIS EYES WERE WAY BETTER THAN MINE, OR MAYBE IT WAS HIS NOSE.
NOT THAT ONE. CRAWLING WITH SKELS.

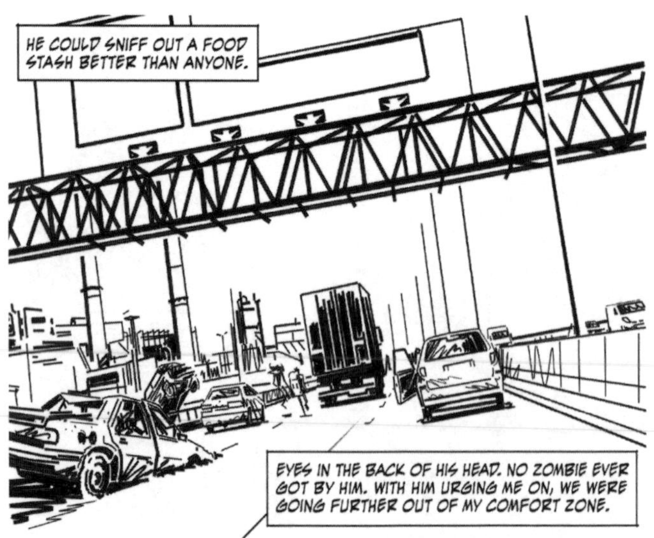

HE COULD SNIFF OUT A FOOD STASH BETTER THAN ANYONE.
EYES IN THE BACK OF HIS HEAD. NO ZOMBIE EVER GOT BY HIM. WITH HIM URGING ME ON, WE WERE GOING FURTHER OUT OF MY COMFORT ZONE.

BILLYBONES MADE ME FEEL SAFE, SO WHEN HE SAID JUMP, I'D DO IT, EVEN IF IT WAS OUT OF A TALL TREE. WOULDN'T BE THE FIRST TIME, AFTER ALL.
SUNSHINE
ELECTRICAL

AND IF BB STARTED POINTING ME TO PICK UP THINGS OTHER THAN CANNED GOODS, WELL, YOU DO FAVOURS FOR MATES, DON'T YOU? EVEN IF YOUR BACKPACK WEIGHS A TON. WHAT'S A FEW...

...ELECTRONIC COMPONENTS BETWEEN FRIENDS?

WHATEVER HE WAS PLANNING, HE DIDN'T FEEL THE NEED TO LET ME IN ON IT. I STARTED HEARING ANOTHER VOICE AROUND THEN, MUCH FAINTER THOUGH, AND THIS ONE SOUNDED LIKE ME. IT STARTED TO SOW DOUBTS IN MY MIND.
WHAT DOES HE WANT WITH ALL THAT STUFF?

IT'S NOT LIKE I HADN'T CHANGED MYSELF AFTER ALL THOSE YEARS. BUT THE VOICE KEPT ON, AT TIMES THREATENING TO BLOT OUT BILLYBONES' VOICE IN MY HEAD.
HE DOESN'T EVEN SOUND LIKE BILLYBONES.

I'D FORGOTTEN THE BIG RULE. TRUST NO FUCKER. LEAST OF ALL A FUCKER I COULDN'T EVEN SEE. HAD TO ADMIT TO MYSELF, I HAD A POINT.

THE NEXT TIME BB PIPED UP, I CONFRONTED HIM - BROUGHT UP THE WOODY'S ORCHARD STORY...
...AND CAUGHT HIM IN A LIE. HE DIDN'T REMEMBER IT AT ALL. THEN IT HIT ME HOW SCREWED UP I WAS. BAD ENOUGH TO HAVE INVENTED AN IMAGINARY FRIEND, BUT TO COME UP WITH SOMEONE ONLY PRETENDING TO BE THAT FRIEND? THAT'S PRETTY FUCKED UP.

I SAID SOME THINGS. HE TRIED TO EXPLAIN HIMSELF, BUT I WASN'T LISTENING. I TOLD HIM I NEVER WANTED TO HEAR FROM HIM AGAIN. END OF.
FINE.

BILLYBONES - WHOEVER HE WAS - LEFT, AND ALL THE VOICES LEFT ME ALONE. ALONE IN A CITY I BARELY KNEW. NOT MY SMARTEST MOVE.

WAKE UP!
WEEKS LATER, I'M JOLTED AWAKE BY A FAMILIAR VOICE; NOT REALLY CLEAR ON WHERE IT WAS I WAS HOLED UP FOR THE NIGHT. OH YEAH, SOME RANDOM FURNITURE STORE. A BED'S A BED.

BLINKING FURIOUSLY IN THE DARKNESS TO WIPE AWAY THE FIREWORK EXPLOSIONS BEFORE MY EYES, I REMEMBERED MY ANGER.
THOUGHT I TOLD YOU TO SLING YOUR HOOK.
YAWN

STAY EXACTLY WHERE YOU ARE.
DON'T PANIC AT WHAT'S ABOUT TO HAPPEN.

BEFORE I COULD THINK OF A COMEBACK, THERE WAS THE SOUND OF BREAKING GLASS FROM ABOVE ME, AND SOMETHING HIT THE GROUND IN FRONT OF ME.

COVER YOUR EYES FOR A MINUTE!

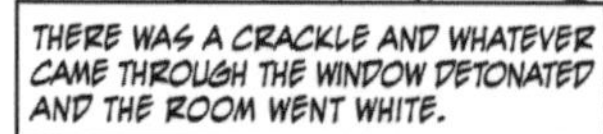

THERE WAS A CRACKLE AND WHATEVER CAME THROUGH THE WINDOW DETONATED AND THE ROOM WENT WHITE.

THEN I SAW WHAT BILLYBONES WANTED ME TO REMAIN CALM ABOUT.

KEEP YOUR HEAD DOWN!
JUMP!

WE HAVE TO GET OUT OF HERE!
WHAT ARE YOU WAITING FOR?

WERE YOU BITTEN? WHERE'S THE BACK-PACK?
ARE YOU INFECTED?

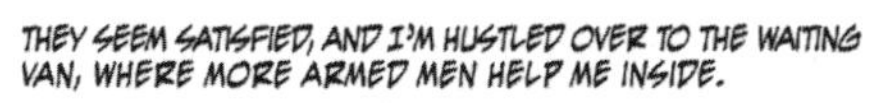
THEY SEEM SATISFIED, AND I'M HUSTLED OVER TO THE WAITING VAN, WHERE MORE ARMED MEN HELP ME INSIDE.

WE ALL SIT ON WOODEN BENCHES FACING EACH OTHER IN SILENCE.

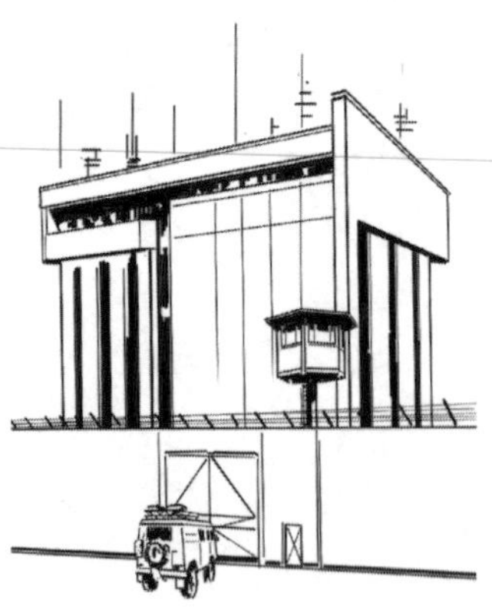
THEY TAKE ME INTO A COMPOUND - THEY CALL IT STORMFORT - TYPICAL SQUADDIES, ALWAYS MAKING UP DRAMATIC NAMES FOR THINGS.

GET YOUR PRIORITIES STRAIGHT! WE WERE THERE FOR THE BACKPACK.
WILL YOU LISTEN TO YOURSELF?
WE'LL GET IT DURING THE CLEAN-UP. THE SKELS WON'T EAT IT, UNLIKE YER MAN THERE.

AT MY DEBRIEFING, THEY TELL ME ABOUT OPERATION INVULNERABLE. THEY'RE TESTING THIS THING CALLED REMOTE VIEWING. MOSTLY, IT MAKES MY HEAD HURT. FAR AS I CAN TELL, THE VIEWER SITS AND THINKS HIMSELF SOMEWHERE, AND REPORTS ON WHAT HE SEES.

PURE FLUKE THEY FOUND ME. THE REMOTE VIEWER WAS OUT HUNTING FOR ELECTRONIC COMPONENTS THEY WERE RUNNING SHORT OF, AND I PINGED ON HIS PSYCHIC RADAR. TO KILL TWO BIRDS WITH ONE STONE, I WAS THEIR PERSONAL SHOPPER TO PICK UP WHAT THEY NEEDED, AND THEY KEPT ME SAFE.
OPERATION INVULNERABLE

WIN-WIN SITUATION.

THAT'S WHEN THE LAST PIECE OF THE PUZZLE FELL INTO PLACE, AND I REALISED WHO THEIR VIEWER WAS.
WHERE ARE MY MANNERS?
THERE'S SOMEONE YOU'LL BE WANTING TO MEET.
NEVER SAID I WAS QUICK ON THE UPTAKE, DID I?

ANOTHER OFFICE LIKE ALL THE REST, BUT WITH TINTED WINDOWS. THE DOOR SLIDER SAID FREE, SO WE WENT RIGHT IN.

BEN! SO GOOD THAT YOU'RE HERE.
I'M SER-GEANT...
THE YOUNG GUY IN ARMY FATIGUES SAT UP FROM HIS COT, AND RAN A HAND THROUGH HIS HAIR.

HIS BROAD SMILE TOOK ME OFF GUARD, GIVEN WE'D NEVER MET BEFORE. AND YET... I STOPPED HIM IN MID-FLOW. BY NOW, I WAS SMILING TOO.
YOU'LL ALWAYS BE BILLYBONES TO ME.

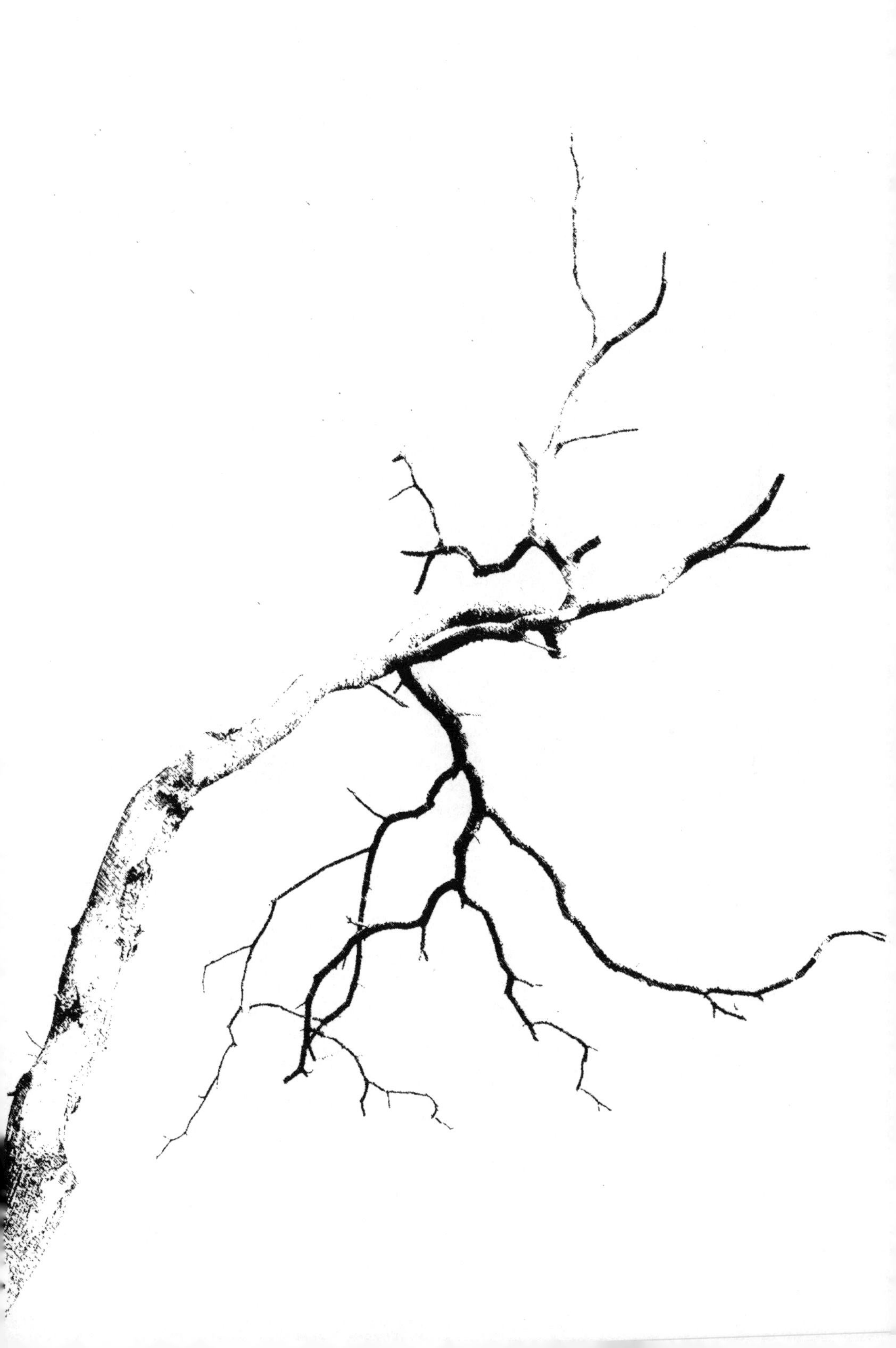

I like the look of that one!
Yeah!!
And that one.
HEPATITIS Z
But that's a bloke?!?
James'll put it in anything Toby!

Aye, Aye lads. I got my sights set.
Yeah me too!
Where? Where?
Over there.

Yeah mate! Mind if I have her friend?
I'm not your Dad Toby, do what you like!
Alright!
See you tomorrow then Jimbo?
Yeah, see ya!

Oh 'ello! You *dancing* with me?
Looks like it don't it!

You got some nice moves...I'm James, can I buy you a drink?
Charlotte. *Vodka, Red Bull* please!

Okay, *cool*, uh...meet you *by* the bar yeah?
I gotta, just uh, nip to the loo!
Right, oh-kaay.
Meet you by the bar?
Mmm hmmm...!

Oh for fu-- *Dave!* Fast work.
murrhgg

Ha! I *know* right!
murr

She's well *wasted* dude, very lively though, *well* up for it...
...got the taste for a *real* man!
murrruhh
Yeah man, go go go!
BANG
BANG
urrrrrrrhhgggg
urhg urhg...
...aagghrrr...
...aagghrrr!!
PSSHHH

oh *yeah* baby...uhr right *there*...uhr uhr
SLAM
urrrrrrr
urghaaaarrghhhh--

Nice one mate...
...I'll see you at home later.
chomp munch crunch

Huh?
Oi! Look, go away!
muuurrruur--

Leave her alone will ya!
THWACK!

uuhhrr

Man, did you see that!? Guy is so wasted he didn't even feel that he broke his--
Oh!

OUT!

mmmmmmmmm
James' flat. Later that night.
mmmm
ooohh
ngg...yeah!
uuhhh

oh
oh, ahhhhhhh
zzzzzz
Uhhhhrrrrrrr
Uhhrrr
zzzzzzzkktt
rr
Uhhhrrrrr
KLANN!
Uhhhrrggg
KLANG!
zzzzzkktt
snort
zzzzzz

uurrhhh
Hey!
Hey! Hey!
Urrhh?
You, uh, went back with James after the club.
Uhhrrrrrrrrr
Is he alright?
Uhhrrrrrrrrrr
Whoa! Did something happen between you and my mate?
mmggggll
mmmffll
Uhhrrrr
Look, not on the street. Let's go into this alley.

mmmm
mggffl
BUY ONE GET ONE
PIZZA
uuhhrrrgh

oh yeah!

oh!
That's different!
oooo!

uurraagghhhhh
ompt
uhhrg
ompt
nomp
uhhrg
chowmpt
mmuhhrgh
chompt

Whoa, *someone's* getting *lucky* tonight!
oooowahhhggggghh
chompt
ompt
nomp
end
KW
2013

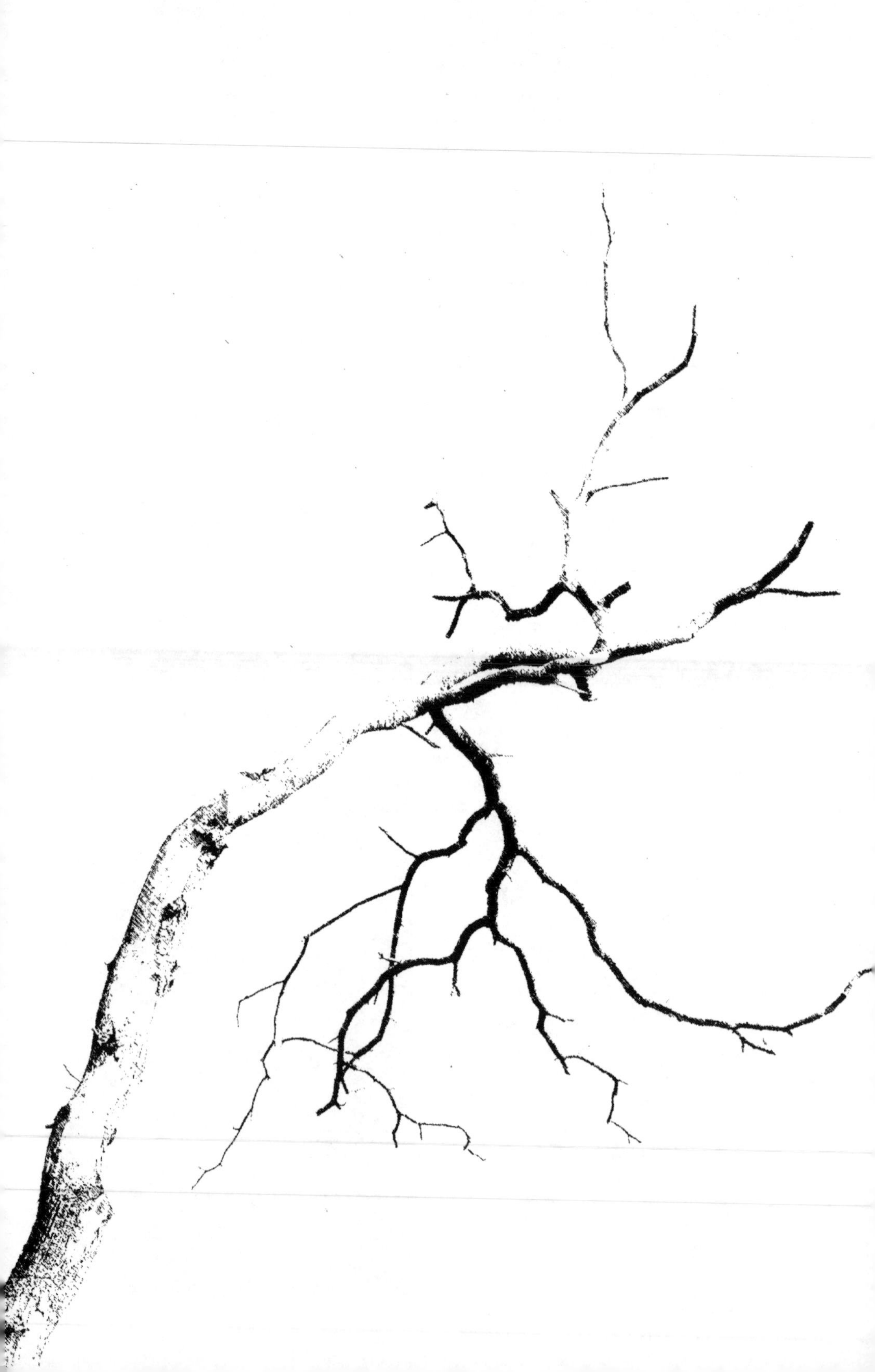

Charlie Parker

STORY BY JOANNA SANECKA DRAWINGS BY DENNIS WOJDA

LIFE IS NEVER WHAT YOU EXPECT IT TO BE. TAKE ME FOR INSTANCE, I WAS BORN TWICE. THE SECOND TIME WAS THANKS TO CHARLIE PARKER.

HM... THAT'S "ORNITHOLOGY".
I MUST BE IN HEAVEN.

(TANK YOU ERIC FOR ALL THE HELP)

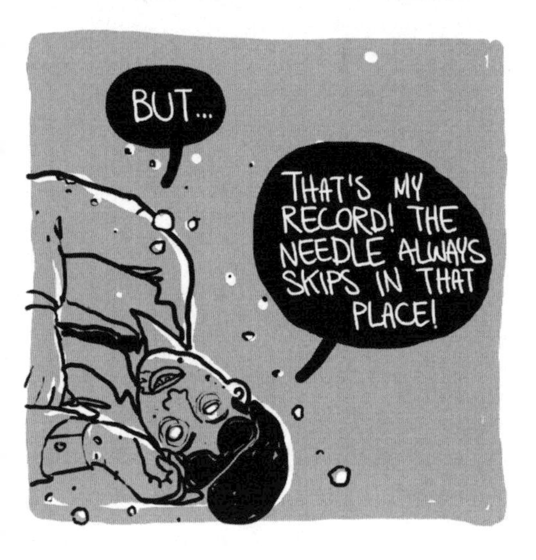

BUT...
THAT'S MY RECORD! THE NEEDLE ALWAYS SKIPS IN THAT PLACE!

WHAT?
WHO THE FUCK IS MESSING AROUND WITH MY CHARLIE PARKER?!

I'M SORRY, I...
IF YOU SCRATCH MY RECORDS I WILL KILL YOU!

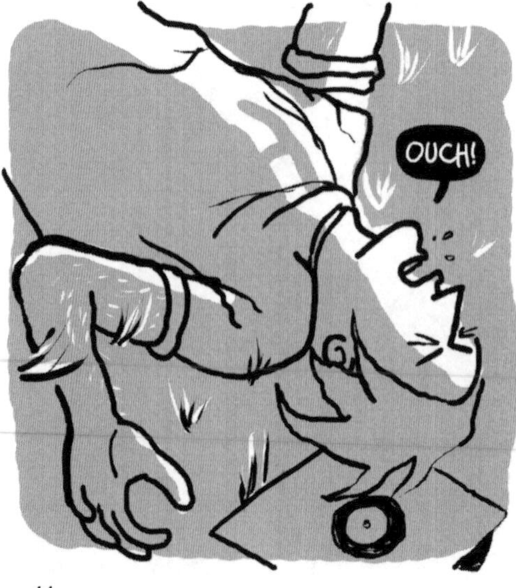
OUCH!

HEY, BUDDY, WAKE UP! I'M SORRY IF I SCARED YOU.
UH...

I HAVEN'T INTRODUCED MYSELF. I'M ROMAN.
ALEX. I THINK... I NEED A DRINK.

TELL ME ALEX, HOW LONG HAVE YOU BEEN LIVING IN MY HOUSE?
YOUR HOUSE? MY FAMILY HAS LIVED HERE SINCE THE FIFTIES.
CHEERS.
SO, WHO BURIED YOU IN MY GARDEN, ROMAN?

THAT'S A LONG STORY.
BY THE WAY, IS LISTENING TO JAZZ STILL ILLEGAL?
NO.

REALLY?
BACK IN MY DAY YOU COULD GET ARRESTED OR EVEN KILLED FOR LISTENING TO JAZZ.

ANYWAY, MY BUDDIES AND I WERE HAVING A PARTY HERE IN THE GARDEN.
IT WAS MAY, 1952
WE WERE JAMMING AND I WAS PLAYING THE SAX.
YEAH.

SUDDENLY, THE POLICE SHOWED UP.
ALL HELL BROKE LOOSE.

WE PULLED OUR KNIVES AND THEY STARTED TO SHOOT.
THAT'S ALL I CAN REMEMBER.

PHEW!
I GUESS THINGS CHANGED FOR THE BETTER WHEN STALIN DIED.

WHAT? STALIN'S DEAD?
YOU'RE KIDDING ME?

LISTEN PEOPLE!
COMRADE STALIN IS DEAD!
HOORAY!
WE DON'T HAVE COMMUNISM ANY MORE.
CALM DOWN, MAN. EVERYONE KNOWS THAT.

I DRINK TO THAT!
IS THERE A GOOD PLACE WE CAN GO TO CELEBRATE?
SURE.

SOMEWHERE THEY PLAY JAZZ.
CLEF RECORDS
YEAH, I THINK I KNOW THE RIGHT PLACE FOR YOU.

WHY DON'T YOU HAVE A CAR, ALEX? I MEAN, THEY ARE SO COOL NOWADAYS. JUST LOOK!
XXIV
HELL

I DON'T LIKE CARS. THEY POLLUTE THE ENVIRONMENT. I PREFER TO TAKE THE BUS OR THE TRAM.
BULLSHIT! PUBLIC TRANSIT IS FOR LOSERS!

HEY, BABY!
ZOMBIE...

CORSO
41
AND THE WOMEN ARE AMAZING TOO. I LOVE THOSE SHORT SKIRTS!

YOU'RE PULLING MY LEG! THE CLUB IS IN THE PALACE OF CULTURE?!
HELL

THEY WERE BUILDING IT BACK IN YOUR DAY, RIGHT?
I HATE IT!

I MEAN, THE SOVIETS BUILT IT RIGHT IN THE MIDDLE OF WARSAW!
WHY DIDN'T YOU TEAR IT DOWN?

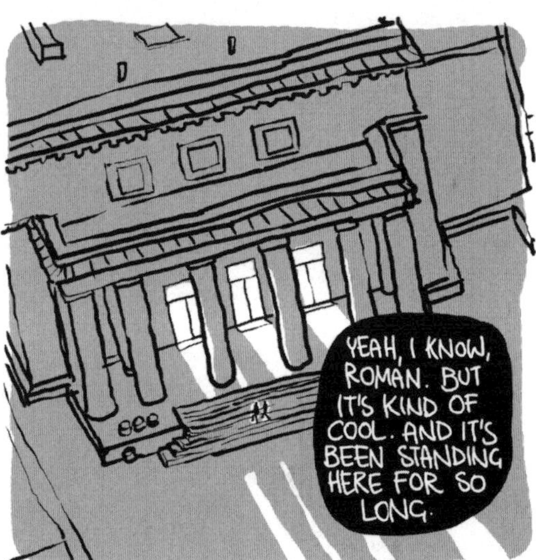
YEAH, I KNOW, ROMAN. BUT IT'S KIND OF COOL. AND IT'S BEEN STANDING HERE FOR SO LONG.

ARE YOU COMING, OR NOT?
JUST A SEC. I NEED TO FIX MY HAIR.
THE BAND HAS STARTED TO PLAY.

LIFE IS NEVER WHAT YOU EXPECT IT TO BE. AND I OWE IT ALL TO CHARLIE PARKER.

THE END

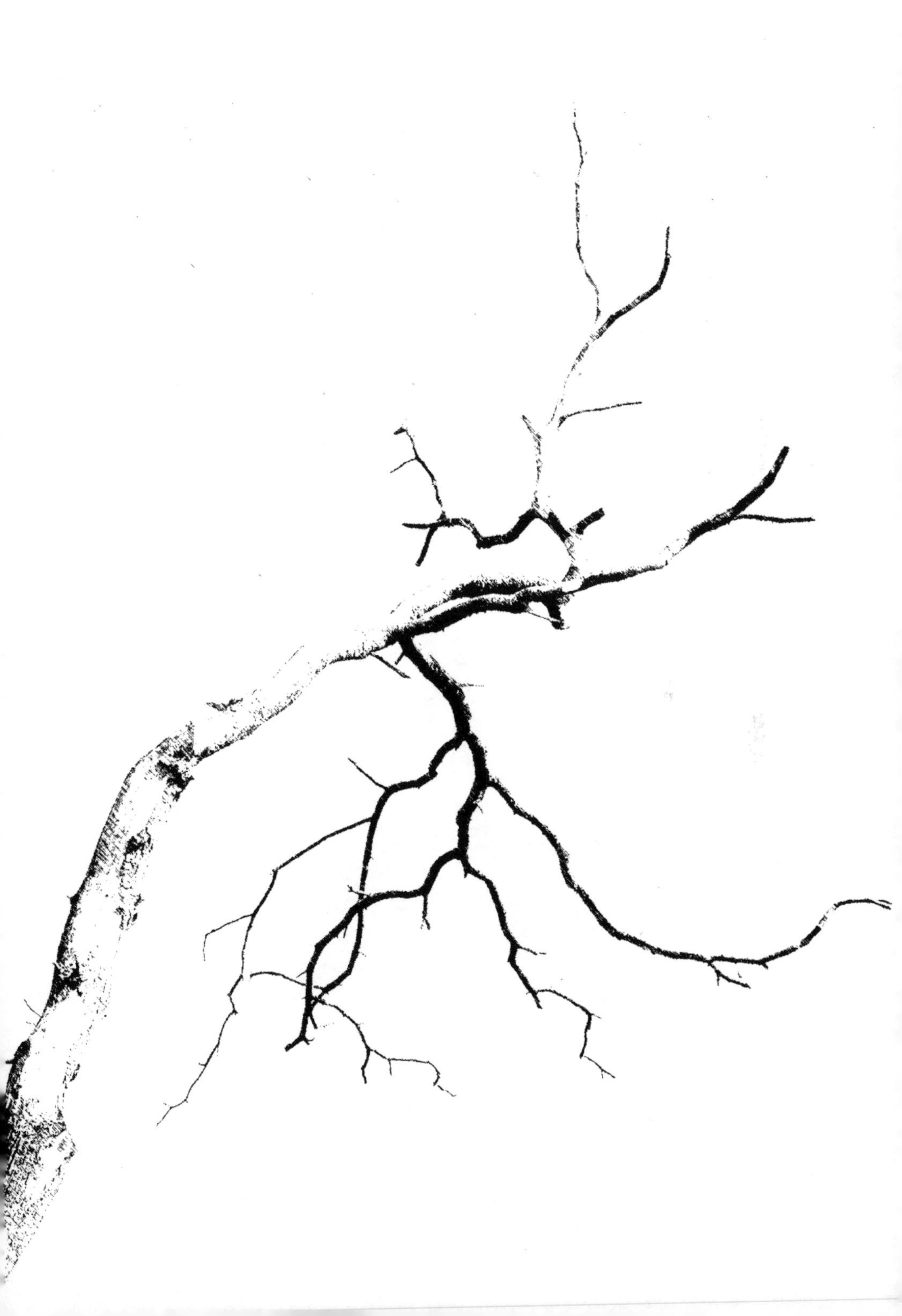

THE DAY THE CURE WAS DISCOVERED-

--OR RATHER, THE DAY THE CURE WAS HASTILY ENGINEERED--
CLICK!
-WAS A TIME OF ELATION FOR MANKIND...
IT WAS SAVED AT THE BRINK OF COLLAPSE.

THE CURE WAS A GODSEND-
--A RAY OF HOPE--
-IN AN UTTERLY HOPELESS AND DEFEATED WORLD...

IT WAS A RECAPTURING OF OUR SPECIES' FUTURE.

THE MONTH PRECEDING THE CURE WAS CONSTANT CHAOS...
A FRIGHTENED, BRUTAL AND VIOLENT TIME OF SAVAGERY:
AMONG BOTH THE LIVING AND THE DEAD.

OF COURSE THE CURE WAS BY NO MEANS AN IMMEDIATE ELIXIR FOR ALL THE CATASTROPHIC DAMAGE OF THAT TERRIBLE TIME.
OPEN LATE
STAR CAFE

OPEN LATE
STAR CAFE
A RECLAIMING OF OUR HUMANITY? YES: BUT THE AFTERMATH OF BLACK JULY CAN STILL BE SEEN TODAY, SOME 2 YEARS LATER.

The Cured
By Nick O'Gorman
BETIVU EUGEN & GORGO

ADMINISTERING THE CURE WAS ONLY THE BEGINNING OF THE TREATMENT.

A SIMPLE AND INTEGRAL STEP, YES, BUT ULTIMATELY A MINOR ONE WHEN CONSIDERING THE REST OF THE WORK THAT WENT INTO "HEALING" THESE BROKEN PEOPLE.
VICTIMS OF BLACK JULY

BETWEEN THE SKIN GRAFTS-
-AND THE PROSTHETIC LIMBS-
VICTIMS OF BLACK JULY
-THE "CURED" PATIENTS WERE QUITE DISTINGUISHABLE FROM THE SURVIVORS IN THIS NEW AGE OF HUMANITY.

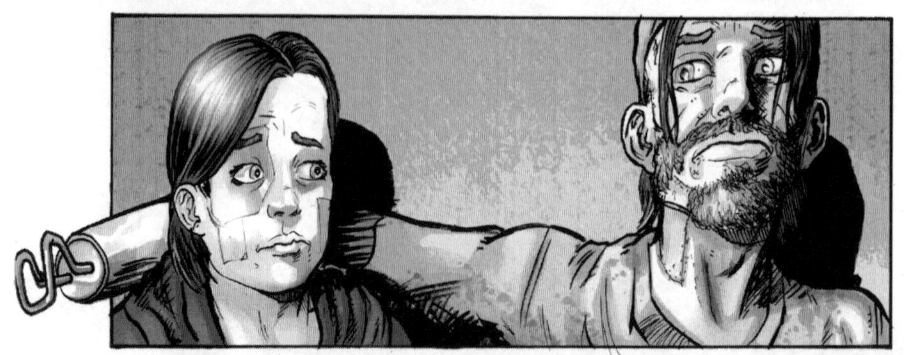

HOWEVER, THESE SUPERFICIAL QUALITIES AND IMPERFECTIONS WERE SECOND TO AN EVEN MORE DISTINGUISHING FACTOR:
THE HAUNTED LOOK IN THE EYES OF THE FORMERLY UNDEAD.

AS MUCH AS THE SURVIVORS WOULD RELISH TO FORGET THE MANY HORRIBLE MEMORIES OF THAT TERRIBLE MONTH-
THEY WEREN'T HALF AS TORTURED AS THE REINVIGORATED-REANIMATED.

THEIR DEATHS, THEIR VICTIMS, AND THEIR MEALS ALL SO EVIDENT BY THE DISTINCTIVE LINES ON THEIR FACES.

THE LINES OF NEAR-SLEEPLESS NIGHTS.
THE LINES OF TORTURED DREAMS.

WHEN SOCIETY HAD ALL BUT TOPPLED, THE FEW SURVIVING GOVERNMENT OFFICIALS AND AGENCIES RUSHED TO BURN ALL OFFICIAL DOCUMENTS-
-ALL RECORD OFFICES, ALL PRESIDENTIAL LIBRARIES.

THEY KNEW THAT THE FUTURE-
--IF THERE EVER WAS TO BE ONE AGAIN--
-WOULD NOT JUDGE WESTERN CIVILIZATION KINDLY; ALBEIT JUSTLY.

AND FOR ALL THE GOVERNMENTAL DOOMSDAY PREPARATIONS, EMERGENCY PROTOCOLS AND DISASTER PLANS-
BANG!

"SELF DESTRUCT IN 3. . .
2. . .
1. . ."
-THE SYSTEMATIC DESTRUCTION OF ALL GOVERNMENTAL RECORDS AND DOCUMENTS WAS THE ONLY ONE THAT WAS SUCCESSFULLY CARRIED OUT.
NATION WIDE.

IN REALITY, THE UNDEAD WERE "CURED" SOLELY TO EASE THE MENTAL STATE OF THE GENERAL POPULATION. FOR THE *SURVIVORS*,
"CURING" THE ILLNESS WAS A SANCTIONED AND CONCERTED EFFORT FROM THE REASSERTED POWERS-THAT-BE TO AID THE TORTURED SURVIVORS IN FINDING SOME KIND OF PENANCE...
5

TO CREATE THE POSSIBILITY OF HOPE.

BITTEN?
REPORT IT IMM
TO REGAIN CONTROL, TO BE RESILIENT.

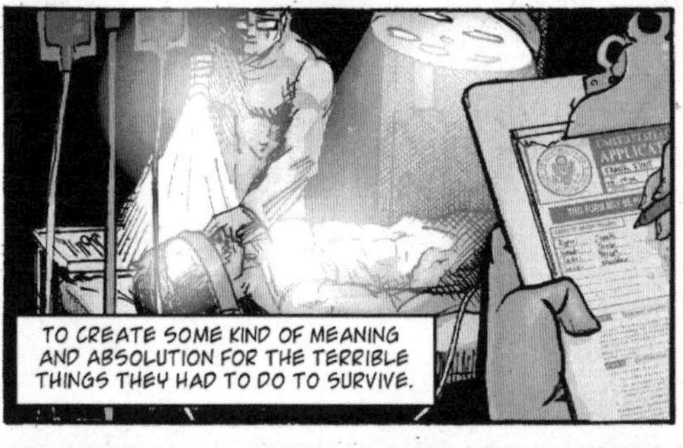
TO CREATE SOME KIND OF MEANING AND ABSOLUTION FOR THE TERRIBLE THINGS THEY HAD TO DO TO SURVIVE.

FRANK FLINT... CONGRESSMAN

THE TERRIBLE THINGS THEY DID TO THE UNDEAD-
-*AND* THE LIVING.
UNITED STATES OF AMERICA:
APPLICATION for PERSONHOOD
03/24/61
FRANK FLINT
CONGRESSMAN
(R)
NJ
THIS FORM MAY BE PHOTOCOPIED - VOID UNLESS COMPLETE INFORMATION IS S
AREAS OF MAJOR TRAUMA

VACCINE PHASE 2
THE TERRIBLE THINGS THEY *STILL* DO...

THE DOCTORS WORKING ON THE TOKEN CURED VICTIMS HAD NO SHORTAGE OF MATERIALS FOR THEIR SKIN GRAFTS.
A GREAT NUMBER OF CAPTURED ZOMBIES WEREN'T ADMINISTERED THE CURE, BUT WERE STILL OF CRUCIAL IMPORTANCE TO THE CURES SUCCESS.
MANY OF THE CURED WOULD CONSIDER THIS A WELCOME ALTERNATIVE.

WELL BEFORE MOST OF THE SURVIVORS HAD REACHED THE 30 DAY MARK OF THAT DREADED MONTH THEY HAD LONG LOST THEIR FORMAL RESPECT FOR THE DEAD.
THEIR UNDERPINNING FAITHS' SHAKEN, THEIR TRADITIONS ABANDONED, THERE WAS LITTLE VENERATION AMONG THE LIVING TOWARD THE DEAD.

WHILE THE SURVIVORS HAD ALMOST UNIFORMLY LOST THEIR REVERENCE OF DEATH RITUALS AND THE LIKE, THE FORMERLY UNDEAD EXALTED THEM ALL THE MORE.

PERHAPS THIS REVERENCE STEMS NOT FROM A SENSE OF MOURNING FOR THE DEAD, BUT INDESCRIBABLE SADNESS TOWARDS THE LOSS OF A LIFE.
JOAN ADAMS
1986-2012
Beloved wife and mother.
AMANTHA ADAMS
2006-2012
WITH THE CURED'S KNOWLEDGE OF THE HOLLOWNESS THEREAFTER, THEY CAN ONLY EMPATHIZE, ESPECIALLY WHEN CONSIDERING THE INEVITABILITY THAT THEY TOO WILL RE-ENDURE THAT SAME FATE.

LUCKILY FOR THE UN-UNDEAD, GUNS ARE MORE ACCESSIBLE THAN EVER IN THIS POST-POST-APOCALYPTIC WORLD.
GUNS
GUN SHOPPE

-AND THE TERM 'FOODBANK' HAS BECOME A LOT MORE LITERAL.
SELF STORAGE
FOOD
BANK
GUNS
INDOOR RANGE
THE GUN STORE

POST

A **THRILLING TALE** from the **ZOMBIE APOCALYPSE** by **NATHAN CASTLE**

THE END

I HAVE LIVED HERE ALL MY LIFE. FOR EIGHTY THREE YEARS I HAVE SEEN FAMILIES COME AND GO. NOW THEY'VE ALL BUT GONE.

FOR
0121 711172
IN SEVENTEEN DAYS, A ONCE VIBRANT COMMUNITY HAS GONE FROM VILLAGE FETES AND YOUNG FARMERS' DISCOS TO UNCERTAIN FATES AND DISEMBOWELMENTS.

I NEVER THOUGHT I WOULD BE ONE OF THE LAST PEOPLE LEFT LIVING IN THE VILLAGE.

Little Med
Parish Chu
Services: Sunday 10:30am
Tuesday 7:30pm
Cemetery and Crematorium
Office hours: Monday - Friday
10:00am - 4:30pm
BUT THEN AGAIN THERE'RE THOSE LIVING HERE WHO AREN'T *ACTUALLY* LIVING ANYMORE.

OLD BILL
DAVE METCALFE-CARR
SCRIPT, ART & LETTERS

MORNING BILL. HOW ARE YOU TODAY?
'OWDO VICAR. I 'AVE T'ADMIT IT AIN'T ONE OF THE BEST DAYS OF ME LIFE.

IS IT ALL READY LIKE I ASKED?
IT IS BILL, IT IS.

NOW, IS THERE ANYTHING ELSE I CAN DO TO HELP YOU?

AYE, VICAR THERE IS.
I'D LIKE T'SET MESEN RIGHT WI' GOD, SO IF I CAN 'AVE A FEW MINUTES...

CERTAINLY. I'LL BE A FEW MINUTES, THEN WE'LL HEAD OFF, IF THAT'S OKAY?

AYE, THAT'S FINE, VICAR.
MY LORD, I WANT TO THANK YOU FOR EVERYTHING YOU'VE GIVEN ME.

YOU PROTECTED ME WHEN THOSE AROUND ME WERE DROPPING LIKE FLIES. THE MOST BEAUTIFUL WIFE AND KIDS. BUT NOW... *NOW* I'M AT A PLACE I *NEED* TO HEAR YOU TELL ME WHAT TO DO.
I *CANT* LET EDIE BECOME ONE OF THOSE...THOSE *THINGS* OUT THERE. I *CANT* LET IT 'APPEN TO 'ER.

BUT I CAN'T FACE SEEING HER KILLED BY SOMEONE ELSE, AND THAT'S WHERE I'M LOST, FATHER.

THOU SHALL NOT KILL, IT SAYS IN T'BIBLE.
I KNOW SHE'S *ALREADY DEAD*, SHE *AIN'T ALIVE* ANYWAY, BUT SHE'S ME WIFE AND I 'AVE TO DO THIS, BUT 'OW CAN I KILL WHAT WERE 'ER WITHOUT BREAKING YOUR LAW?

I *PROMISED* TO 'ONOUR AND PROTECT EDIE, AND I'VE DONE THAT FROM DAY WE WED. THIS IS *THE ONLY WAY* I CAN STILL DO THAT.

BUT IT MEANS GOING AGAINST *YOU* LORD, AND I SAID I'D *NEVER* DO THAT. SO, AM I GOING T'BE DAMNED F'KILLING SUMMAT THAT'S DEAD *ALREADY*?

AND SO WE HEADED OFF THROUGH THE MAZE OF UNEARTHED GRAVES TO THE FAR SIDE OF THE CREM'.
ALL THE TIME, THE ONLY THOUGHT GOING THROUGH MY HEAD WAS "DON'T LET ME BE TOO LATE."
OKAY, VICAR. NOT TOO FAR TO GO.
WE SHOULD HAVE THIS DONE BY TE---
OH MY LORD!
MMMRRRRHH
NOT QUITE, JUST ONE OF HIS SERVANTS.
BLAM
MMRREEEIIIIL!

BLIMEY! I NEVER THOUGHT I'D BE SHOOTING MR CRAVEN FROM THE POST OFFICE!

HE ALWAYS OVERCHARGED ANYWAY, VICAR. AND HE WAS 'AVING IT AWAY WI' JUDY PEGG AN' THEY WERE BOTH WED.

MORE IMPORTANTLY, 'OW DOES A MAN OF T' CLOTH BECOME SUCH A CRACK SHOT AND 'AVE A GUN IN HIS POSSESSION?

BEFORE I TOOK HOLY ORDERS, I WAS STATIONED IN NORTHERN IRELAND DURING THE TROUBLES. THIS WAS FOR MY PROTECTION AFTER I WAS DEMOBBED.
THAT'S WHERE I LEARNT TO SHOOT MOVING TARGETS. IT'S ALSO WHERE I FOUND A NEW GENERAL AND A NEW BATTLE TO FIGHT.

WELL, VICAR, YOU'D BEST GET THAT SHOVEL OFF YOUR BACK---

WE'RE HERE.
IN LOVING MEMORY OF
EDITH EDIE
ELAINE CHUBB
BORN 16 JUNE 1927
PASSED ON 29 MARCH 2013
AGED 82.
LOVING DAUGHTER,
MOTHER AND WIFE

I DON'T MIND DOING THE DIGGING IF YOU WANT ME TO BILL.
YOU'RE ALL RIGHT, VICAR, I NEED TO DO THIS MYSELF.
THANKS THOUGH,AND THANKS FOR AGREEING TO THIS. I KNOW IT CAN'T BE EASY FOR YOU.
WELL, NO TURNING BACK NOW.
WHUNK!

IN LOVING MEMORY OF
EDITH EDIE
ELAINE CHUBB
BORN 16 JUNE 1927
PASSED ON 29 MARCH 201
AGED 82.
LOVING DAUGHTER,
MOTHER AND WIF
HHHRRRRRMMMM!
WE STOOD ROOTED TO THE SPOT AS WHAT WAS ONCE EDIE CHUBB CRAWLED OUT OF THE HOLE SHE WAS BURIED IN.
BUT THIS WASN'T EDIE CHUBB. EDIE CHUBB HAD DIED FROM CANCER BACK IN MARCH, AND HAD GONE TO BE WITH HER MAKER.
THIS WAS A JUST SOME SOULESS PUPPET THAT HAD TAKEN OVER WHAT WAS LEFT OF HER BODY.
HELLO EDIE, MY LOVE.
MY GOD, HOW I'VE MISSED YOU.
HHHRRRRRMMMM!
HHHRRRRRMMMM!

OH, MY EDIE. I'VE COME TO TAKE YOU HOME.

HHHRRRUMMH

HHRRRRLLLHHH

HHHRRRRROOOWWWWWLLL!
YYAAAAARRRRGGHH!
VICAR, DO IT! DO IT NOW!

PLEASE. RELEASE HER FROM THIS.

I'M SORRY, BILL. I'M SO SORRY.

BANG

SETH & GHOST VS:
ZOMBEASTS
by JAMIE LEWIS
DESTROY THEM
OF COURSE, MY MASTER
MINIONS!
PRODUCE THE CARRIER OF PESTILENCE!
PLEASE...
AAAAA AAAA A
ARGH!

THE NEXT DAY:
THEY'RE RIGHT BEHIND ME! I THINK THEY ATE MY WIFE!
HI, MAYOR JUST-A-BRAIN! WHAT'S GOING ON?
!!!
!!!
!
!
STOP
ZOMBEASTS!
BRAIN?

GHOST, STOP! WE LEFT PYRAMID CAT BEHIND!
HE'S 90% BRICK, HE'LL BE FINE. WE HAVE TO GET YOU TO SAFETY.
DON'T WORRY GHOST! I HAVE A PLAN...
HELP...
... AND ONE OF THESE!
BUZZ
WOW! I THOUGHT SKULLBEES WERE EXTINCT. GOOD LUCK!
FIGHT!
OK THEN... I'M GOING TO LET YOU OUT BUT ONLY IF YOU DO ME A FAVOUR. FIND THE WIZARD, OK?
>SIGH< OK, BUT YOU OWE ME PAL.

HEY, CASSETTE BOY! WE COULD USE YOUR HELP.
S... E... TH
N... EE... D... BA... TT... ERY ... O... VE... R ... TH... ERE...
GRRR
DR TRAPEZOID? NOT YOU TOO! STAY BACK...
!
KRASH
PLEASE BE QUICK, SETH. THEY JUST KEEP EATING ALL OF OUR FRIENDS.

ZAP ZAP!
OK, ZOMBEASTS, LET'S GET THIS OVER WITH.
YOU THINK YOU'RE WINNING? THIS CHANGES NOTHING. ARISE, MY FINAL MINION!
STOP

ROAR!
I SURRENDER..?
BOSS STAGE:
GIANT ZOMBEAST FIST-TONGUE
UMM...
POIK
WELL GHOST, I SUPPOSE THIS IS IT.
WE TRIED OUR BEST.
GR
YOU WERE GREAT, SETH. I'M PROUD OF YOU.

WELL AIN'T THIS THE CUTEST THING YOU EVER SAW?
I DID WHAT YOU SAID KID. THE WIZARD'S RIGHT BEHIND ME.
YAY!
HEHEHEHE
OH...
I HOPE YOU CAN SWIM, YOU LITTLE BRAT. THAT'LL TEACH YOU TO KEEP ME IN A JAR FOR SIX MONTHS!
HEALING TIDE OF
DEX'MAK'NAR!
STOP

THANKS MR WIZARD!
WHERE AM I?
I SAVED THE DAY SO YOU MUST PAY. IT'S TIME TO GO, I OWN YOUR SOUL!
GONE
PING
COULDN'T YOU HAVE FOUND A LESS ECCENTRIC WIZARD? I LIKED HAVING A SOUL.
FIND YOUR OWN SAVIOUR NEXT TIME, YOU LITTLE SNOT.. I'M OUTTA HERE.
AND YOU STILL OWE ME.
CURSE YOU SETH AND GHOST!
WAIT! I HAVE TO GET TO WORK... THE CHILDREN!
HA HAHA HA HAHA!
ENJ

Horrific wails fill Belfast. The undead seek flesh
ELCOME
O BELFAST
POUND SHOW
OF FLESH
Few places are safe. The brave and the mad dash from one refuge to the next
Some rush with messages or are simply lost and avoiding the bite of the undead horde
ZOMBIE BITES SO HARD TO BEAT
What are ye running for!
Please! Please keep it open!
Oh Sweet Jesus They're Everywhere!
Get in you eidjit !
Someone needs to sort these 'uns out, like !
Be our guest, big bollocks!

DID YOU GET BITTEN?
DID THE COLLEGE SEND YOU?
ARE THEY STILL HOLDING OUT?
I . . . I DON'T KNOW ABOUT ANY MESSAGES
WHO ARE YOU? IDENTIFICATION NOW!
MR. MICHAEL JONES
SOCIAL SERVICE
COMMUNITY RELATIONS
PLEASE, I'M JUST LOOKING FOR MY GIRLRIEND, SUZY
GREAT. JUST WHAT WE NEED. A SOCIAL WORKER. GIVE ME A BREAK, LIKE!
I GUESS YOU THINK THEY'RE JUST MISUNDERSTOOD MONSTERS?
JEN TAKE IT EASY. I HAVEN'T HEARD OF A SUZY
WE ARE GETTING READY FOR EVACUATION. WE NEED ALL THE HELP WE CAN GET
THERE'S THREE STRONGHOLDS LEFT. HOPEFULLY SUZY GOT TO GO OUT WITH THE FIRST EVACUATION
WELCOME TO DZD DIE ZOMBIE DIE!
CATCHY ISN'T IT ? ROLLS OFF THE TONGUE
WE DON'T HAVE MUCH AND NOT MUCH WORKS
IT COULD WORK MAYBE . . .

How's it looking, Jim. We near good to go?
It Could Work Eoin. Maybe
It'll work! It'll work!
I can't leave without knowing for sure if . . .
If what? If She's Dead? Or worse?
We've all lost someone Some more than others
My son and my daughter. Both were.. Both were bitten
I couldn't do it. I watched them . . . change
God forgive me. I wish they were dead
I'm . . . I'm so sorry, Eoin

FORSTER ZOMBIE KILL
EVIL DEAD II
CRASH
I AIN'T GOING ON ANY MAYBE!

LOOK. IF SHE GOT OUT FORSTER GREEN IS THE BEST BET. THAT'S IF.

YOU TELL ME RIGHT NOW. CAN THIS WORK?
WELL . . .

WE ARE HEADING PAST THERE BUT FIRST WE HAVETO GET TO THE TRANSPORT POINT
WE WILL NEED HELP, MICKEY

IT COULD WORK! MAYBE!
MAYBE!
AARGH!
C.H.

IF YOU CAN GET ME THERE, I'LL DO WHATEVER IT TAKES
I HOPE YOU FIND HER. I REALLY DO. NOW GET SOME REST. BELFAST WILL BLAZE AT DAWN

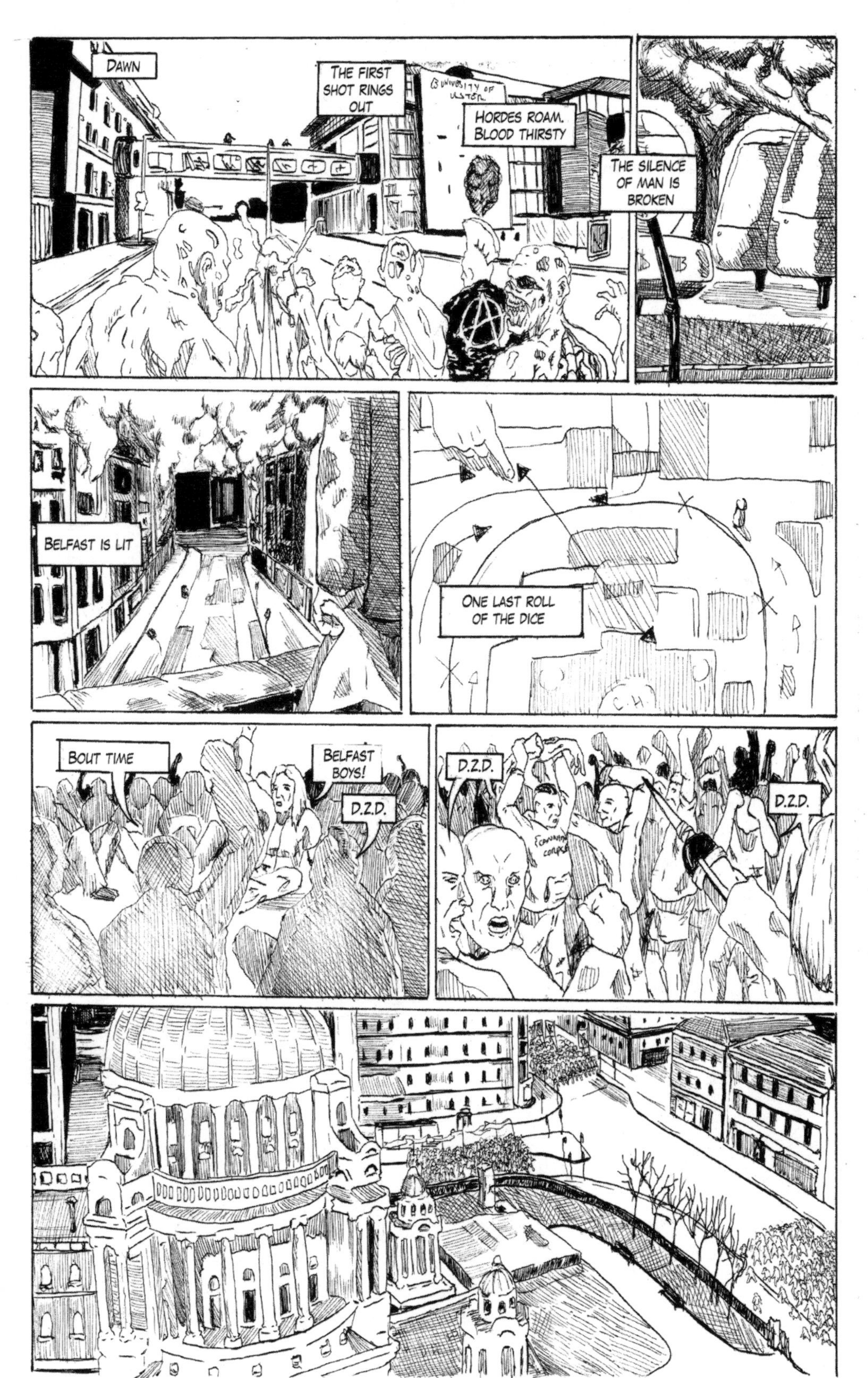
DAWN
THE FIRST SHOT RINGS OUT
UNIVERSITY OF ULSTER
HORDES ROAM. BLOOD THIRSTY
THE SILENCE OF MAN IS BROKEN
BELFAST IS LIT
ONE LAST ROLL OF THE DICE
BOUT TIME
BELFAST BOYS!
D.Z.D.
D.Z.D.
D.Z.D.

TO BELFAST
LIVE &
LET DIE

ALL ABOARD STEVE'S WILD RIDE!
L.O.L
DEATH EXPRESS
D.Z.D

I SWEAR THAT DEAD CHICK IS GIVING ME THE EYE
DON'T PISS OFF THE DRIVER

FOR GOD'S SAKE LOVE. I DON'T WANT YOUR FECKIN' BUS PASS!
WHO WANTS A DRINK?

I'M COMING, SUZY I JUST HOPE I'M NOT TOO LATE . . .
ARE WE CRAZY FOR BRINGING A CHILD INTO ALL THIS?
SMICKER WUZ HERE
WE SHALL SOON SEE
K.O.N.T
KISS

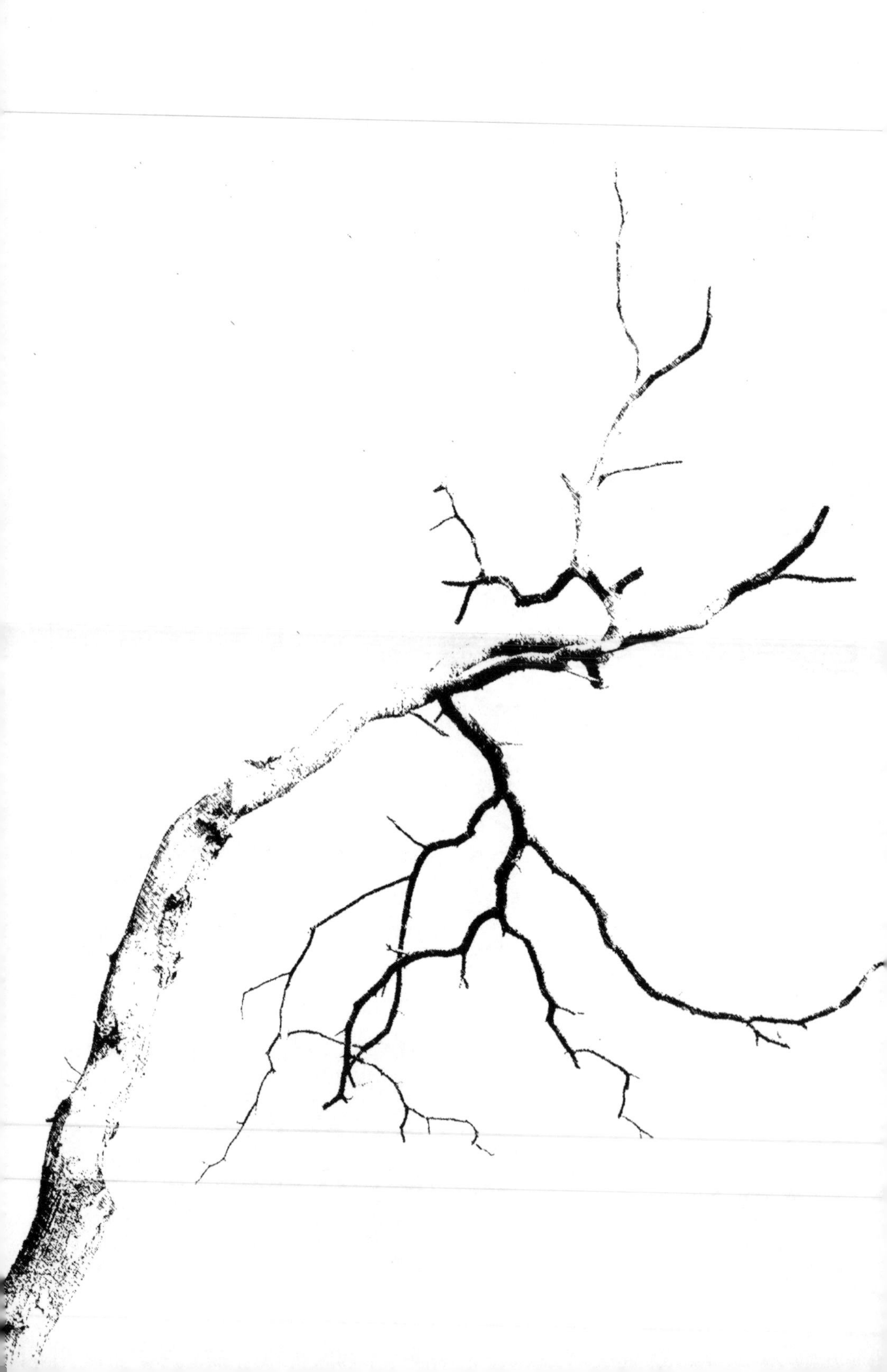

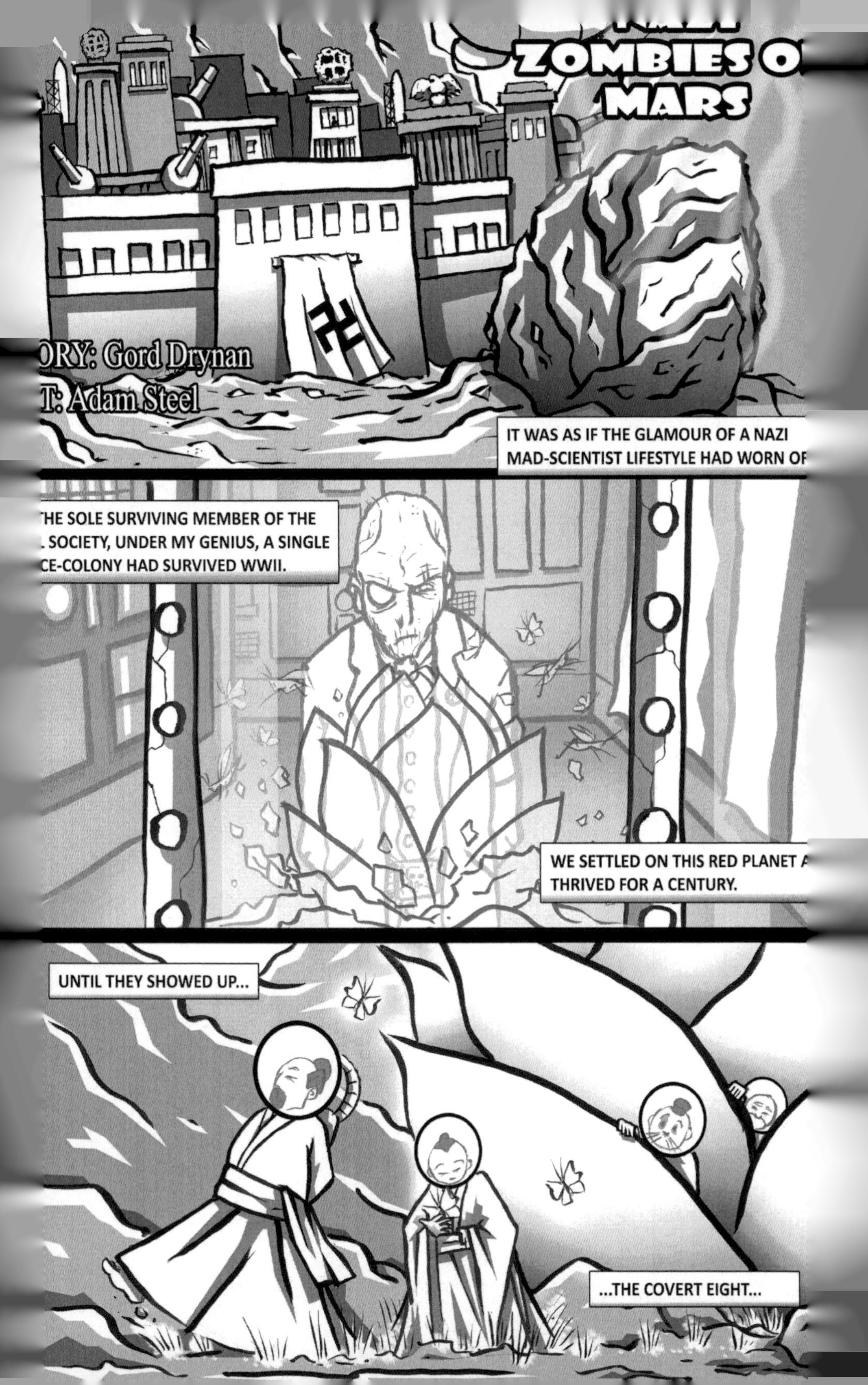
ZOMBIES O
MARS
ORY: Gord Drynan
T: Adam Steel
IT WAS AS IF THE GLAMOUR OF A NAZI MAD-SCIENTIST LIFESTYLE HAD WORN OF
THE SOLE SURVIVING MEMBER OF THE
SOCIETY, UNDER MY GENIUS, A SINGLE
CE-COLONY HAD SURVIVED WWII.
WE SETTLED ON THIS RED PLANET A
THRIVED FOR A CENTURY.
UNTIL THEY SHOWED UP...
...THE COVERT EIGHT...

...THE IMMORTAL SPACE MONKS.
YESTERDAY THE ONLY THING I WAS AFRAID OF WAS MY DAILY CALORIC INTAKE, AND PERHAPS RUNNING OUT OF RIDICULOUS SUPER-WEAPONS TO INVENT.

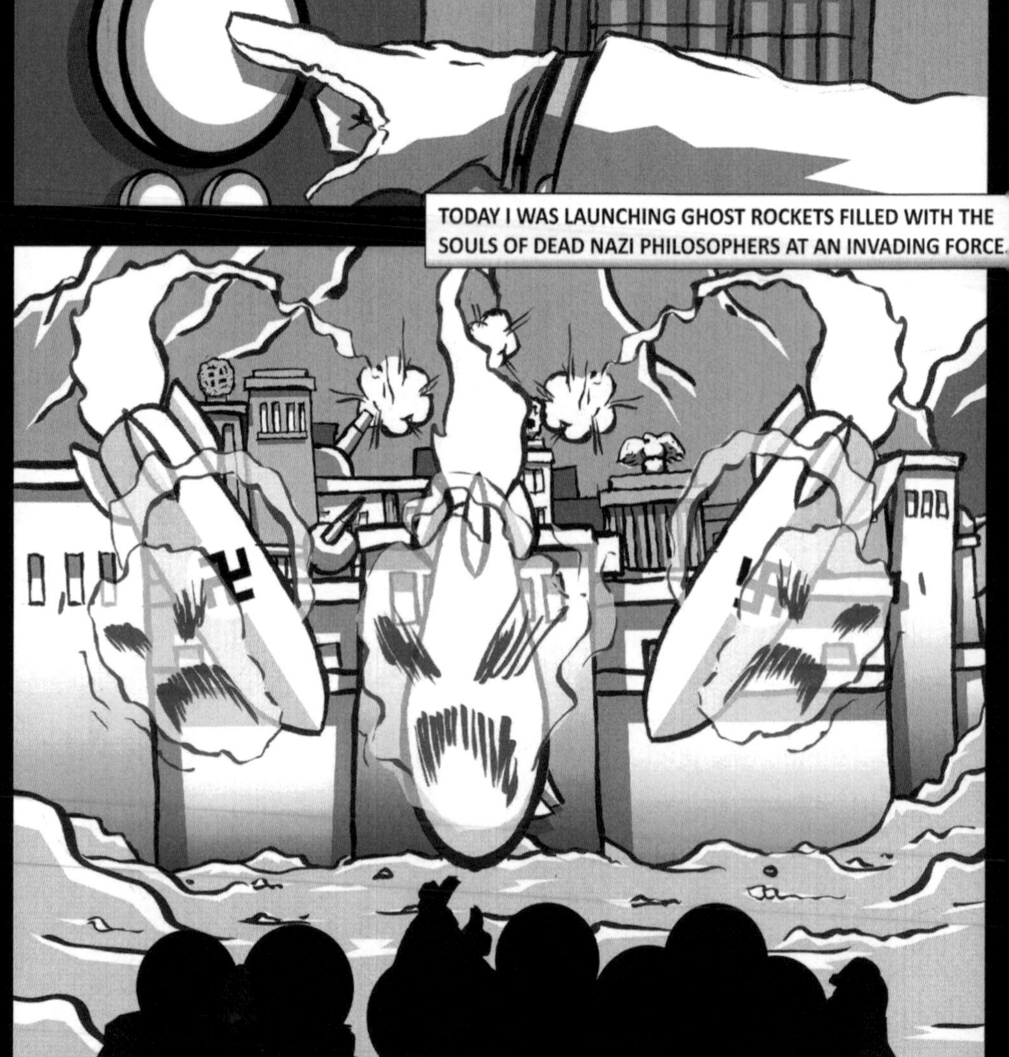
TODAY I WAS LAUNCHING GHOST ROCKETS FILLED WITH THE SOULS OF DEAD NAZI PHILOSOPHERS AT AN INVADING FORCE.

THE APPARITION MISSILES HIT A WALL OF COMPASSION, AND WERE FREED FROM THE WHEEL OF KARMA...
...BUT MORE IMPORTANTLY, MY SPECTRAL AMMUNITION WAS NOW EXHAUSTED.
THEIR LEADER TOOK A BREATH FROM HIS AEROSOL NEBULIZER, WHICH DELIVERED A HIT OF CONCENTRATED ENLIGHTENMENT TO HIS BUDDHIST LUNGS.
THEN HE EXHALED, AND WAVE AFTER WAVE OF ASTRAL BUTTERFLIES RUSHED TOWARDS US, FOLLOWED CLOSELY BY THE TEN TIGERS OF CANTON, WHO RAVAGED THE DEFENSES OF OUR CAPITAL CITY.
AFTER THE HOLY LIGHTNING DESTROYED WHAT WAS LEFT OF OUR COMMUNICATION MATRIX, I PUSHED THE BIG RED BUTTON THAT WE MAD-SCIENTISTS ALWAYS SEEM TO HAVE.

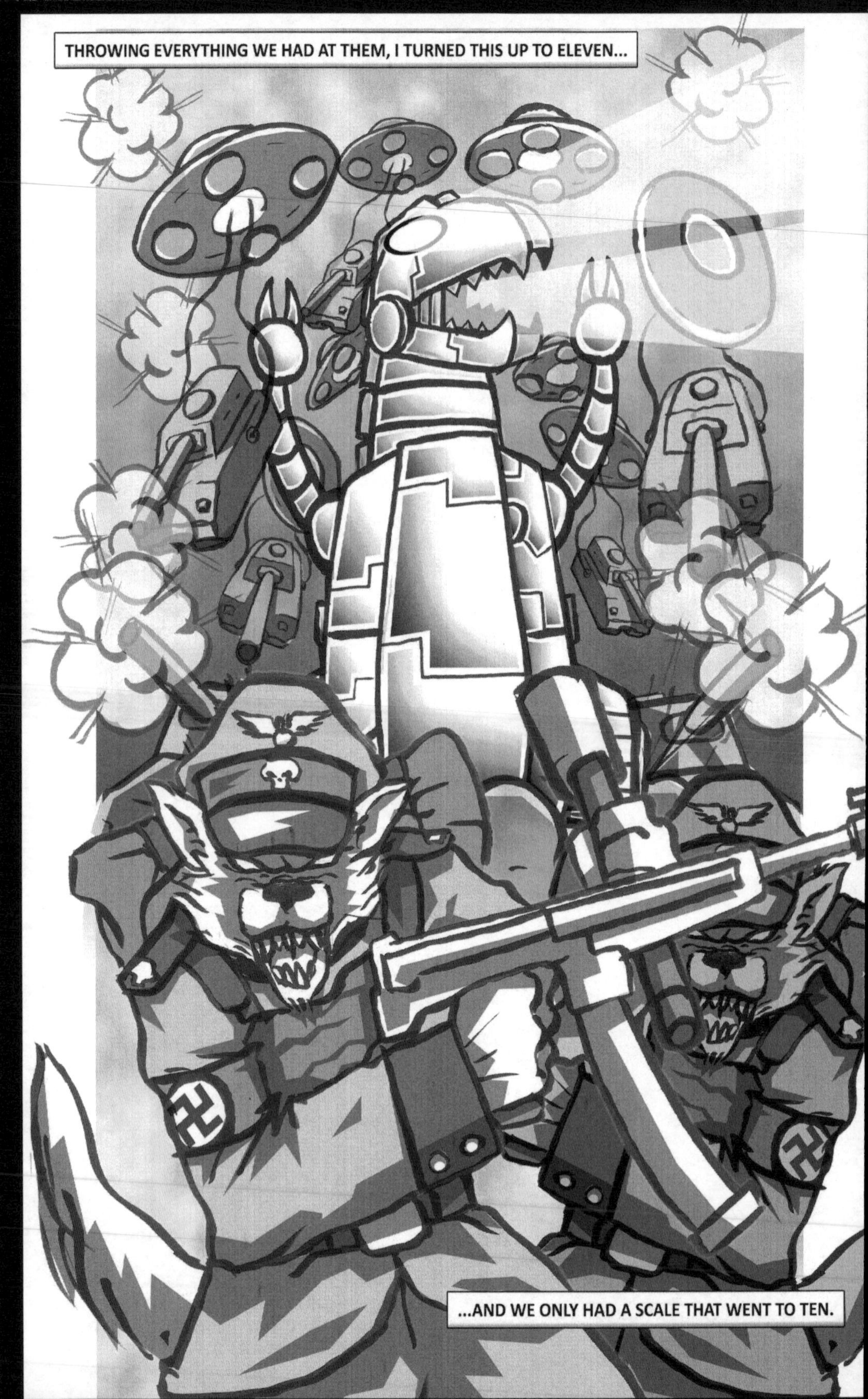
THROWING EVERYTHING WE HAD AT THEM, I TURNED THIS UP TO ELEVEN...
...AND WE ONLY HAD A SCALE THAT WENT TO TEN.

TEN THOUSAND YEARS
WORTH OF KNOWLEDG
AND UNDERSTANDING
EMERGED IN THE FORM
OF SHENLONG, THE SPI
DRAGON.
HELD BACK TEARS
S MY BEAUTIFUL
MONSTERS WERE
ECIMATED BY THE
VERWHELMING
MIGHT OF THE
RANSCENDENTAL
OVE-RAIN THAT
HOWERED
NLIGHTENMENT
OWN UPON THEM.
THEY HAD
WEAPONISED
LOVE, AND WE
HAD NOTHING
TO DEFEND
AGAINST IT.

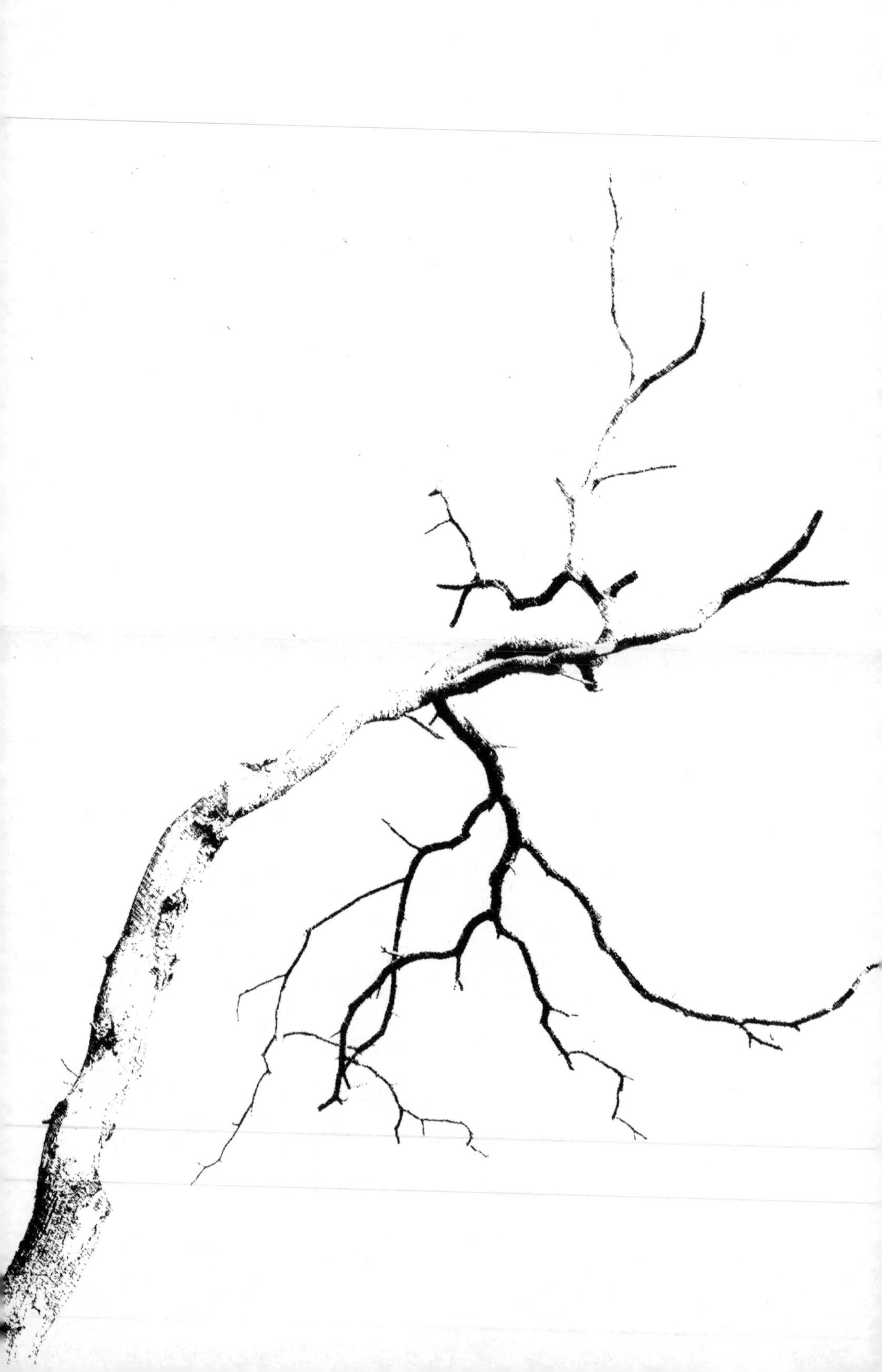

Finally a day off.

THAT'D BETTER BE MY *KICKSTARTER* REWARD, I'VE BEEN WAITING AGES FOR IT.
RENT-IT
STEVEN HEWITSON
25A PLUMMER ST
MAIDSTONE
KENT
OVERDUE

HMM, *RENT-IT!* I HAVEN'T BEEN IN THERE FOR MONTHS---

RENT-IT
75 QUID! FOR 'THE BUSINESS' AND 'FOOTBALL FACTORY'-- THAT HAS TO BE A MISTAKE!
tson
advised that your account
y £75 in arrears, due to the films
ow not being returned.
Entertainment LTD
Business
all Factory

DAMMIT, MY HAND HURTS!--

TALKING TO YOURSELF AGAIN STEVEN? FIRST SIGN OF MADNESS YOU KNOW!

This guy is my worst nightmare, lets himself into my flat all the time
HA, NO MORNING MR PRITCHARD JUST GOT A BILL FOR SOMETHING I NEVER BOUGHT.
YOU GOT MY RENT YET?--

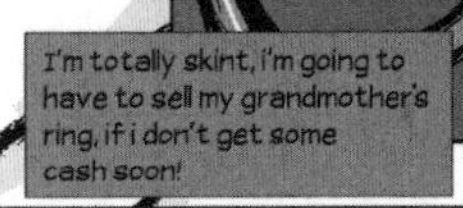
I'm totally skint, i'm going to have to sell my grandmother's ring, if i don't get some cash soon!

I'M REALLY SORRY MR PRITCHARD, I DON'T HAVE YOUR RENT YET. I'M WORKING ON IT!

THAT'S 2 WEEKS LATE NOW STEVEN, I LIKE TO COLLECT MY RENT PROMPTLY, I DON'T DEAL WITH LOSERS. NOT A LOSER ARE YOU STEVE?--
WHAT HAPPENED TO YOUR HAND?
SOME CRAZY GIRL BIT ME ON MY WAY HOME FROM WORK LAST NIGHT!

WELL, IT LOOKS LIKE SHE'S NOT THE ONLY PERSON WHO WANTS A PIECE OF YOU!
BUT BEAR IN MIND, IF YOU HAVEN'T GOT MY RENT ONE WEEK FROM TODAY, IT WON'T BE YOUR HAND I'LL BE CHEWING ON!-- I'LL RIP OUT YOUR HEART AND EAT YOUR GUTS! UNDERSTOOD?!
YES MR PRITCHARD, UNDERSTOOD!

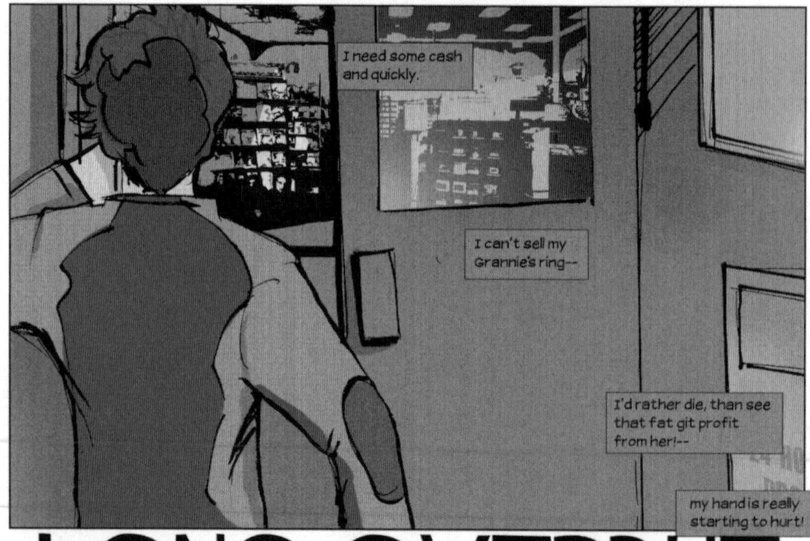

I need some cash and quickly.
I can't sell my Grannie's ring--
I'd rather die, than see that fat git profit from her!--
my hand is really starting to hurt!

LONG OVERDUE

WORDS AND PICTURES BY PHIL BUCKENHAM

AHEM!-- EXCUSE ME.

S'UP?

ERM, I GOT THIS LETTER AND I--
COMPLAINT?
UM, YES!
VERDUE

URGH--

BARRRRY!

HI, BARRY STORE MANAGER HOW CAN I HELP?

I GOT THIS LETTER. IT SAYS I OWE 75 POUNDS
AH, SO YOU'VE COME TO PAY YOUR BALANCE THEN?

NO, I DIDN'T RENT THE MOVIES LISTED, IN FACT I HAVEN'T BEEN HERE FOR MONTHS! I THINK YOUR SYSTEM MAY HAVE MADE A MISTAKE!

OUR SYSTEM DOESN'T MAKE MISTAKES! SO THAT'LL BE 75 POUNDS OR YOU WON'T BE ABLE TO RENT FROM US ANYMORE,
PLUS YOUR CREDIT RATING WILL BE DOWNGRADED AND A COLLECTIONS AGENT MAY BE CALLED TO YOUR ADD--
FRANK

THEY'RE IN THE DRAWER!
AH!

IT SEEMS WE HAVE MADE A BIT OF A MISTAKE
PLEASE FEEL FREE TO RENT ANY FILM YOU WANT FOR FREE

ERM, I DON'T REALLY WANT TO RENT ANYTHING... OK DO YOU HAVE BEN AFFLECK'S NEWEST FILM?

URGH BEN AFFLECK, YEAH HANG ON I'LL GO AND GET IT FOR YOU.

I'm not surprised that company is going down the pan--

ARGHH WHAT...

What's happening to me, my stomach it's burning!

My hand! Wha-- what's happening to me!?

Need to get to my phone--
Need... help
I can't feel my hands!
This is it, this is how it ends--
I'm dying--
Alone!

STEVEN!! ARE YOU IN THERE?
IT'S BEEN TWO WEEKS! YOU NOW OWE ME A MONTH'S--
RENT!
-COUGH- -COUGH-
OH MY GOD!

STEVEN!
-GASP- HE'S DEAD!
I SHOULD CALL THE POLICE OR AN AMBULANCE--
HE IS A MONTH IN ARREARS THOUGH!
HE MUST HAVE SOMETHING OF VALUE IN THS DUMP!
HA HA PAYDIRT! THIS MUST BE WORTH A PRETTY PENNY

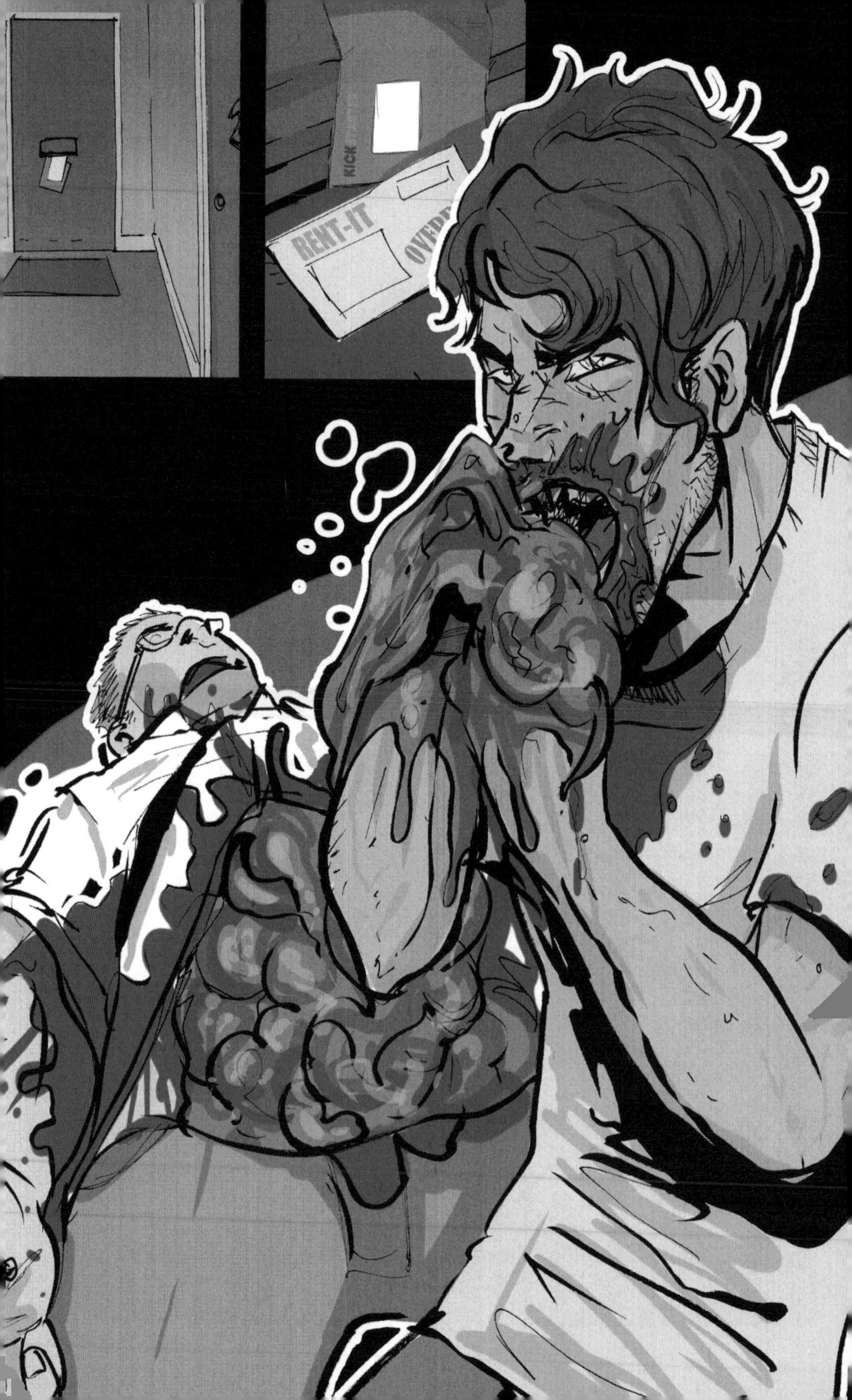
KICK
RENT-IT

LUNCHTIME!
By Peet!
A NEW TERM AT ST. GOVE'S ACADEMY...
HI! GOOD HOLIDAY?
MM-HM!
YEAH, NOT BAD!
OKAY, IF YOU'RE IN KS1 AND YOU'RE IN KS2, I'LL DO THE HALL, THEN JOIN YOU.
MDSA ROTA.
MONDAY
KS1
KS2
TUESDAY
WEDNESDAY
THURSDAY
FRIDAY
WET PLAY
OH, APPARENTLY WE HAVE A NEW LAD TOO, SO WE'LL HAVE TO SEE HE SETTLES IN.
HE'S CALLED....
OTTO.
OKAY, YEAR 5 HOT DINNERS! LINE UP 'QUIETLY', THANK YOU!!

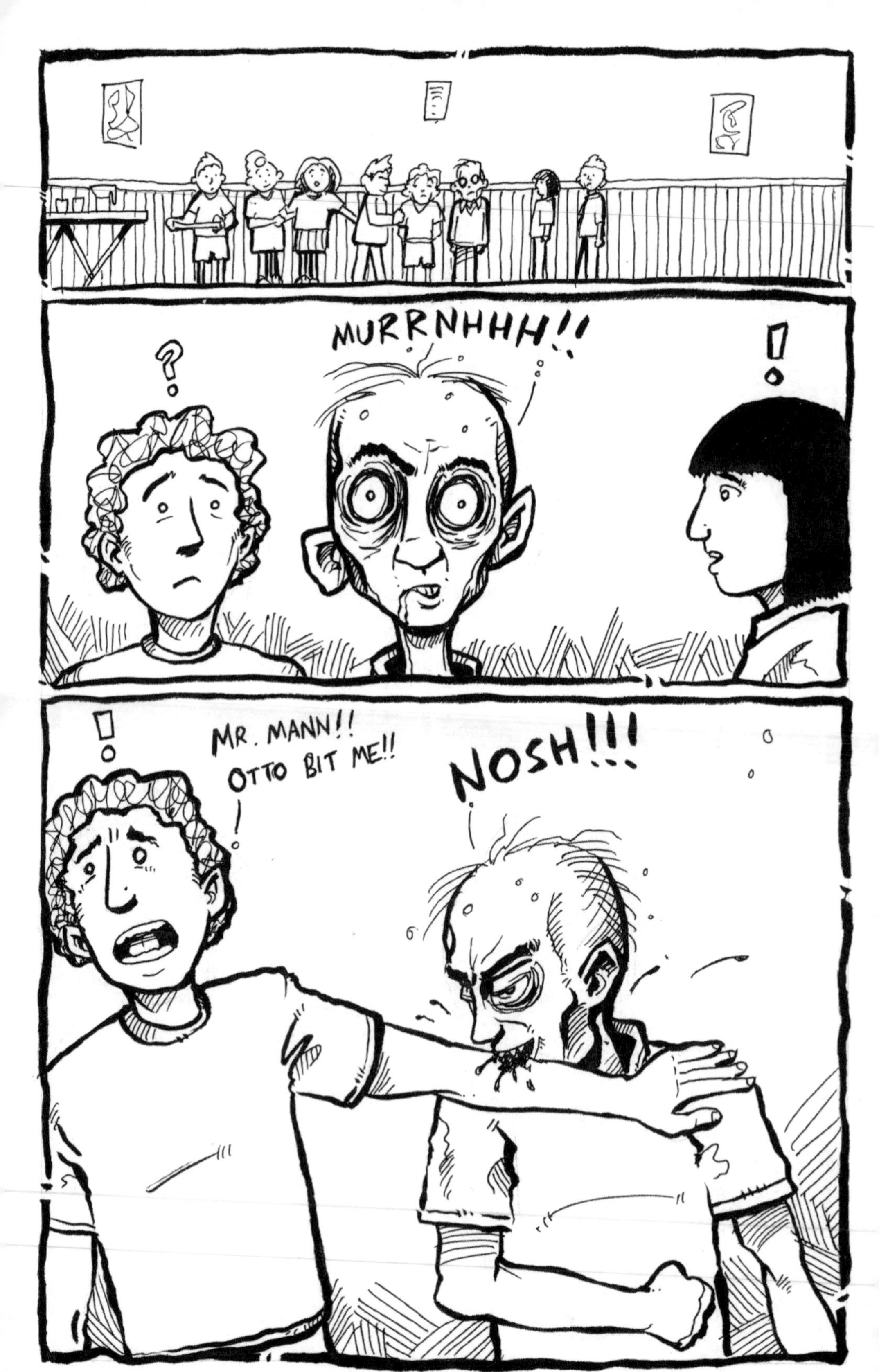
MURRNHHH!!
?
!
!
MR. MANN!!
OTTO BIT ME!!
NOSH!!!

THAT'S NOT HOW WE BEHAVE!
NO BITING, OTTO!!!
ARE YOU OKAY, BENNY?...
MNNHHM..!
BENNY! NO!!!
WE DON'T FIGHT BACK!!!
BOYS!! STOP IT!!!
BENNY! WHAT 'ARE' YOU DOING?!! LINE UP!!!
WOULD YOU LIKE TO GO AND DO THE KS2 PLAYGROUND INSTEAD, MR. MANN?...
SIGH, OKAY...
OH... CRAP!
CAN WE GET THE EQUIPMENT OUT, MR. MANN? PLEEEZ!!
YESS, OKAAY! GO ON THEN!
YAY!!

HOCKEY STICK!!!
WAIT! DON'T RUSH ME!
NO! THAT'S NOT HOW WE USE THE EQUIPMENT!

THIS IS HOW...
WE USE IT!
NAAARRGHH!!
SETTLE DOWN!!
GUHHRK!!

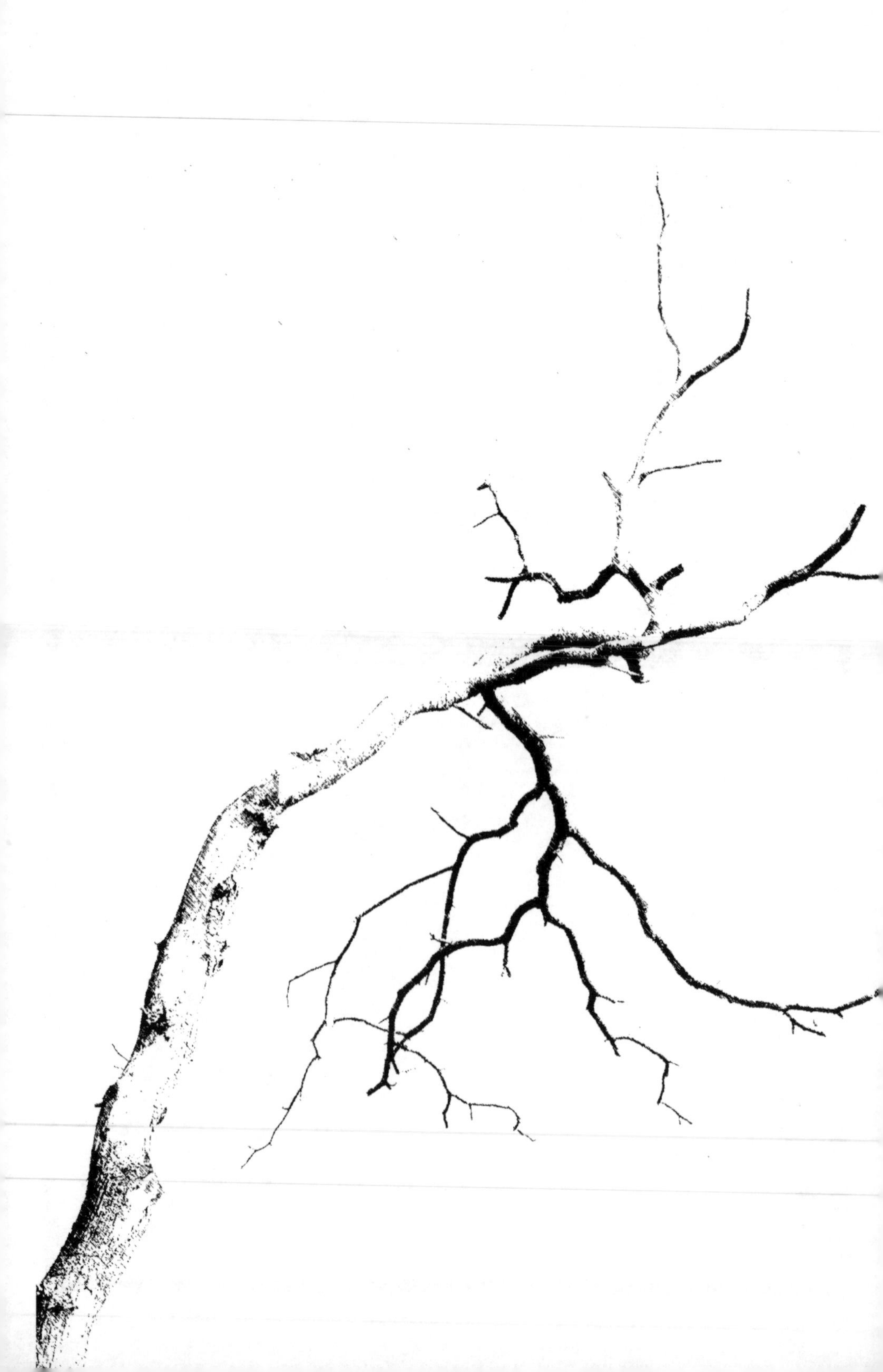

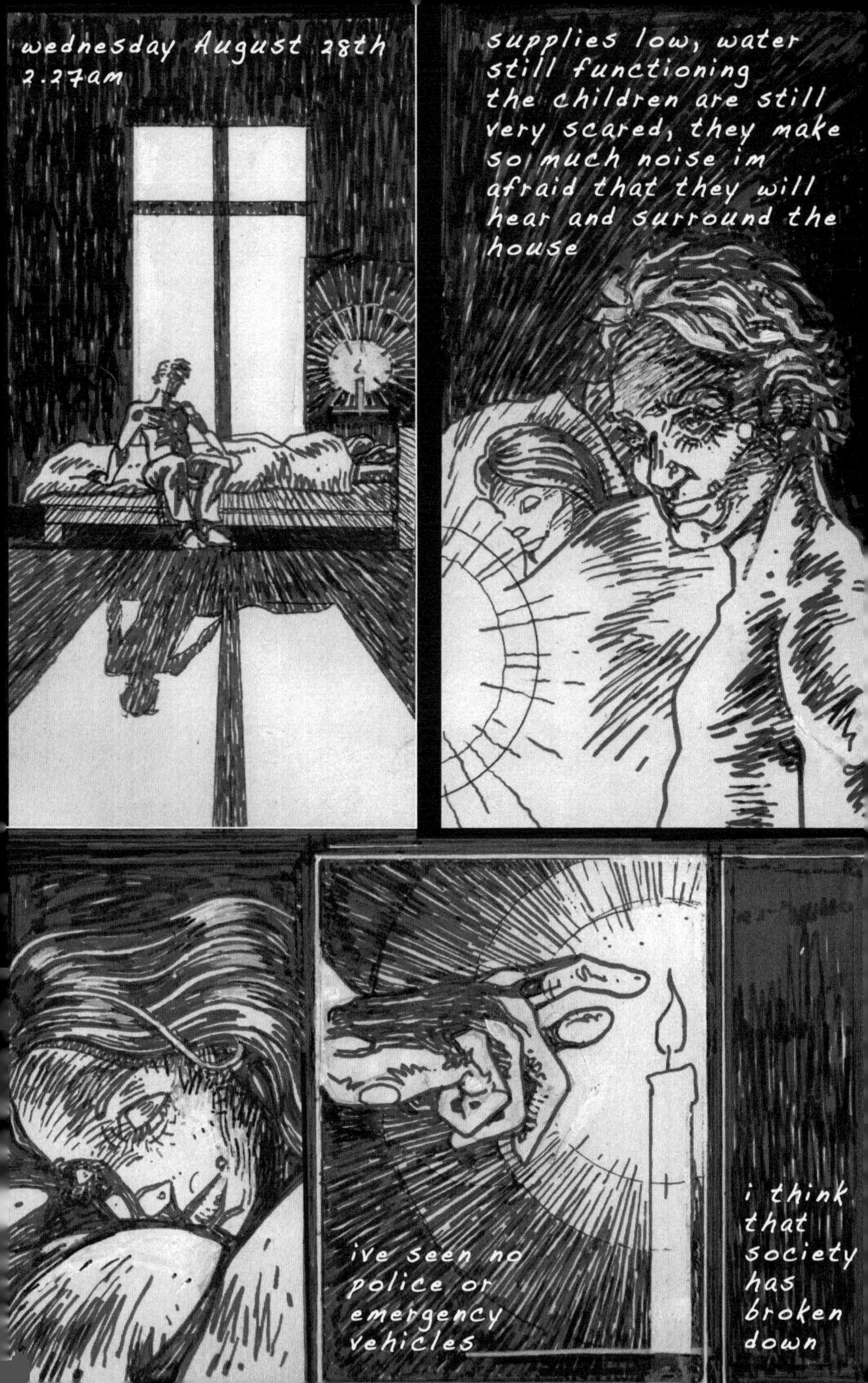

wednesday August 28th
2.27am
supplies low, water still functioning the children are still very scared, they make so much noise im afraid that they will hear and surround the house
ive seen no police or emergency vehicles
i think that society has broken down

No sign of armed forces, the last person died 4 days ago
we are on our own

Family Man
WRITER BADEN JAMES MELLONIE
ARTIST RICHARD WHITAKER

thursday
august 29th
5am
the number of creatures in the close has risen.

Im transporting food and supplies at night to the vehicle. I can only move at night now, its too dangerous

only move at night now, its too dangerous
during the day. Margaret is holding it together
well. her strength guides me and gives me hope
that somehow everthing will be alright,
although ultimately i fear for us all

morning
couldn't sleep?

be careful... please, if its too difficult just come back. we can try again tomorrow
i will love. i'd better get going

i love you

all clear then... good

– lets get this show on the road

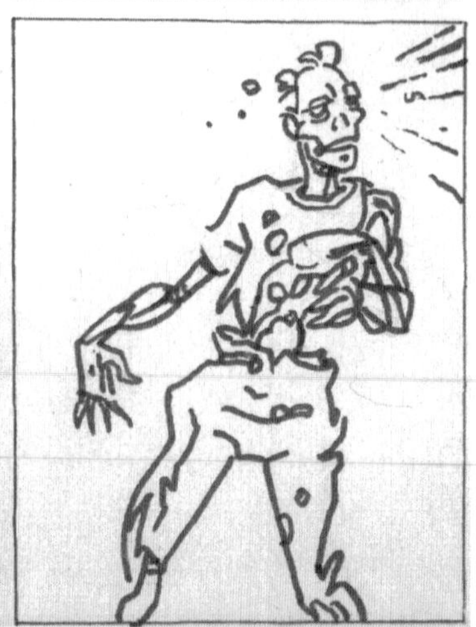

fuck it !

leave now
diary and keys
in bag
i love you
all x

SO, THIS ONE DAY IN JUDEA...

as discovered by Nigel Lowrey

with typography by Tony McGee

...so then I got off the slab, removed the rock sealing my tomb from within and came out to find you guys!
Isn't that cool?

Uhhhm... I dunno really...

Whaddaya mean, y'dunno?!
I just came back, not from the bazaar, but from the dead...

That's like, the coolest thing ever!!

Yeah, but you're all, like..a zombie 'n' shit now, innit?

I am not a zombie... and anyway, that concept hasn't even been formulated yet!

Don't you start your fascist linear time shite with me, Yeshua. You were dead. Now you ain't.
You. Are. A. Fucking zombie. Just like Lazarus Lowenstein.

First of all, he wasn't dead, just comatose because he couldn't handle that Moroccan stuff he'd been smoking.
I was dead but now I'm alive. Zombies are dead people walking about mindlessly and cannibalising random other people...

Well, that's a generalisation... but if you were dead and now you're undead... does that make you a vampire, then?

Oh, for dad's sake!!

Am I gulping down blood, am I? No! Bloody Gehenna, have you no fershlugginer brains?
Yeah...but you can't eat them...

We should write this shit down, it's hysterical...
Oy, who can write? We'd have to trust others to write it down and they'd only cock it up...
Yeshuah could end up looking like a Greek god and having superpowers or something ...

Y'know, dad's right: you really are all a buncha muppets!!
Screw you guys, I'm going home!

Ooh, handbags!
Yeah, but I think if I'd just been crucified, I'd be cross...
2000-ish years later...

Bloody hell!! It's only the soddin' zombie apocalypse!! Run for your lives!

Aargh!!

Blarrhrr!!

No, nnnnahhhrr!!
Ow!

›huff‹
›huff‹
...nearly safely home!!

`kinell! "Let's go out for a bite", she says! Sod that for a game of soldiers!!
Hopefully I can ride this out now!
Wonder if there's anything on TV...?

Might be able to catch that French-
oh, no! noooo!!!

Friggin' Ada, No, no!!
The Cranberries
Besides, you don't wanna eat me, I just had a vindaloo so you'd only regret it in the morning...
Oh, this is really it! Oh God, oh Jesus, help me!
No! Screw you! Now you know what a zombie really is, you can kiss my hairy kosher arse!
Ahhrr!! But... what about..ouch!... forgiveness?
Yeeahhhrblurrggh!!
Do as I say, not as I do...
Fin

milos kuntz presents the stick zombies in:

zennui

an existential crisis

nnnnnnnn

Sigh

uuuuuh

aaaaahnnn

all this moaning is okay, I suppose

braaainzz

but I'd kill for a good conversation

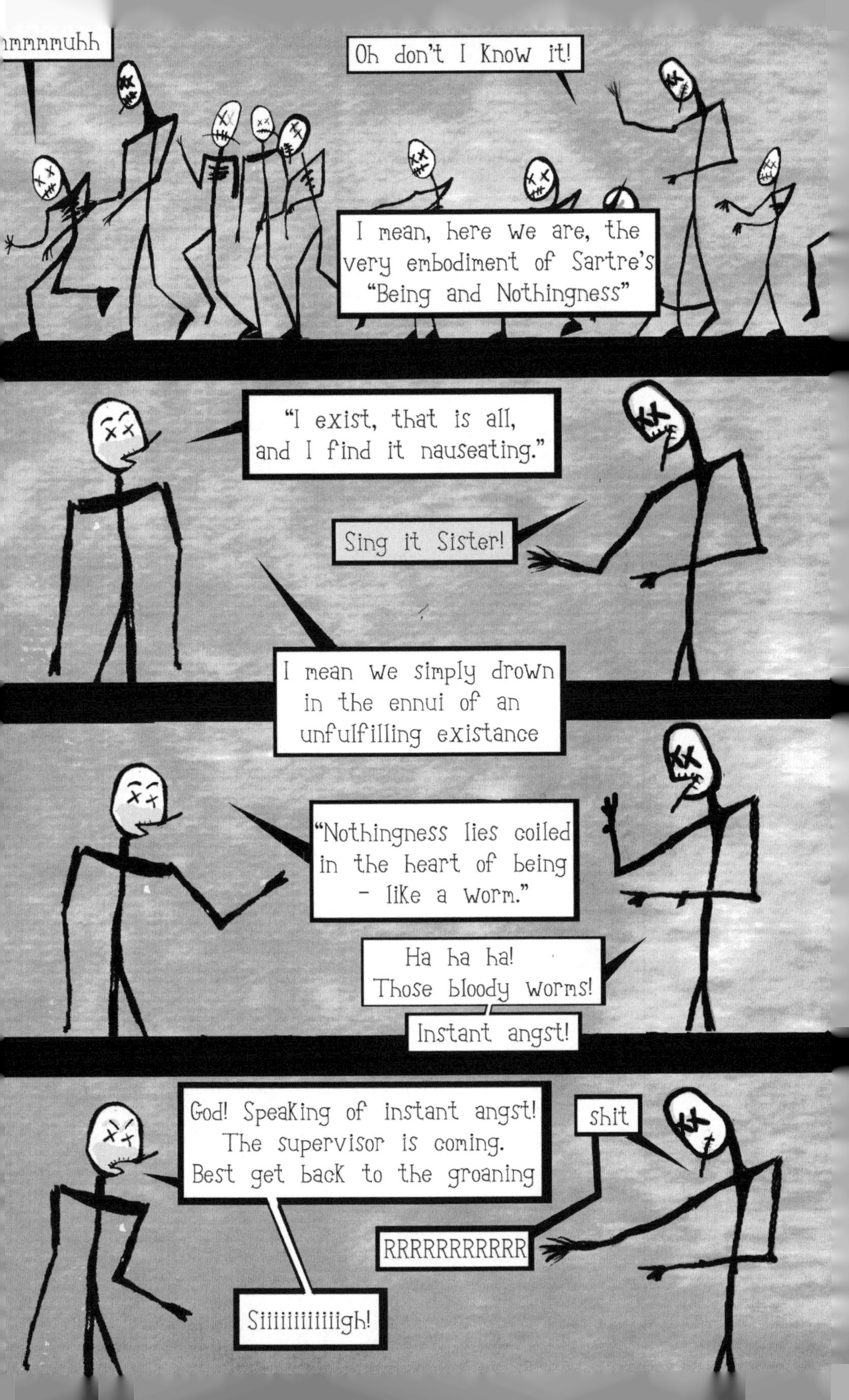

mmmmuhh
Oh don't I Know it!
I mean, here we are, the very embodiment of Sartre's "Being and Nothingness"
"I exist, that is all, and I find it nauseating."
Sing it Sister!
I mean we simply drown in the ennui of an unfulfilling existance
"Nothingness lies coiled in the heart of being - like a worm."
Ha ha ha! Those bloody worms!
Instant angst!
God! Speaking of instant angst! The supervisor is coming. Best get back to the groaning
shit
RRRRRRRRRRR
Siiiiiiiiiiiigh!

Snrf
IN AN APOCALYPTIC FUTURE WHERE EVERYTHING IS REALLY SHITTY, ONE WOMAN ROAMS THE LANDS LOOKING FOR VALUABLE MEDICAL SUPPLIES WHILE BEING CHASED BY THE FEARSOME Z-REX. THIS IS THE
NURSAPOCALYPSE
SKREEE

URRRR
VVIMM

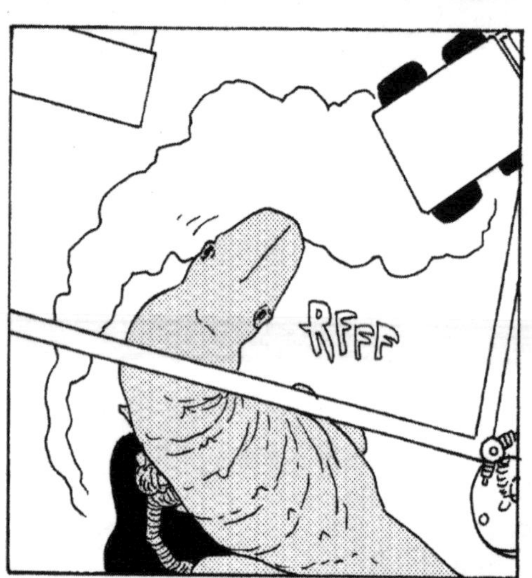
RFFF

URRRRR

HA! YOU SO DUMB AND CONFUSED!

OOPS

KRASH

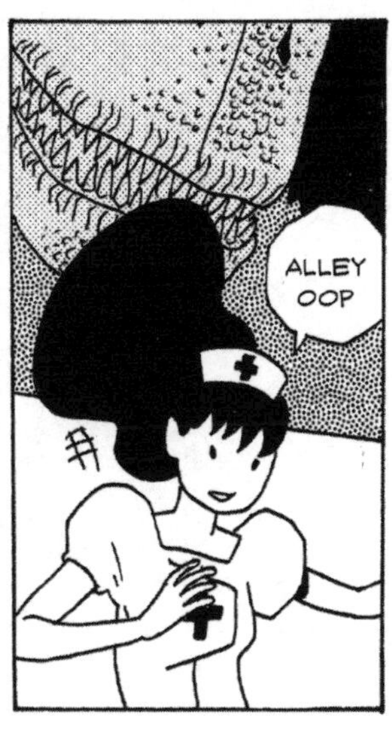

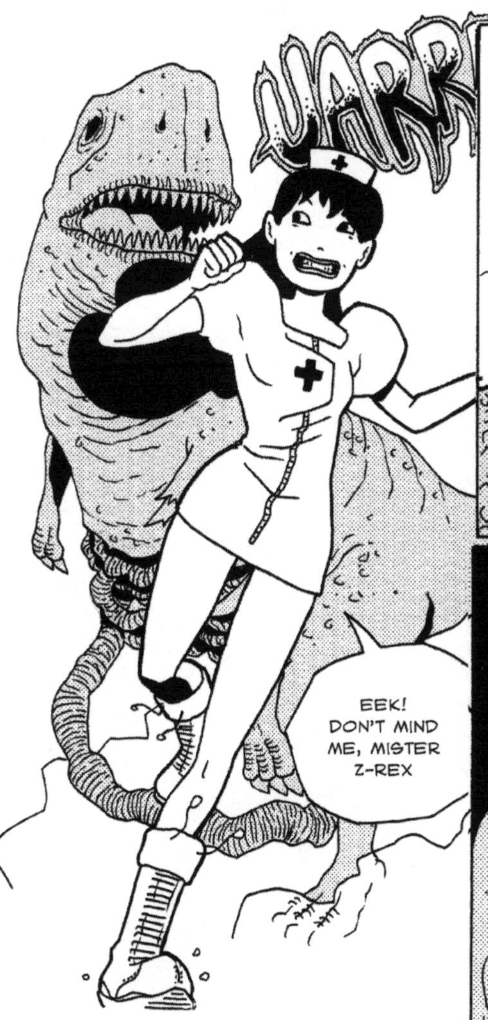

LATERS, TWINKLE TITS

WELL, AS LONG AS EVERYBODY DECIDED TO CLEAN UP AFTER THEMSELVES
BOOP BEEP BOOP BEEP
BOOP BEEP BOOP
FSSH
CODE ACCEPTED. WELCOME BACK NURSE #57253
THAT'S MY NAME, DON'T WEAR IT OUT
EEEY JACKPOT LADIES N' GERMS
dink!

OH!

WELL LOOKY HERE NOW!
HEHEEHEHEE HELLOOO NURSE!

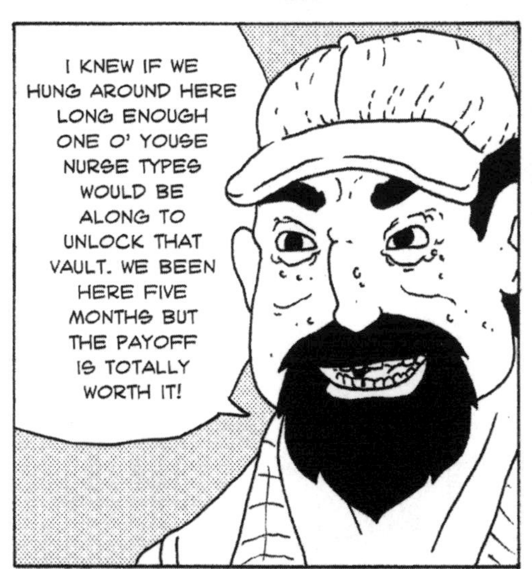
I KNEW IF WE HUNG AROUND HERE LONG ENOUGH ONE O' YOUSE NURSE TYPES WOULD BE ALONG TO UNLOCK THAT VAULT. WE BEEN HERE FIVE MONTHS BUT THE PAYOFF IS TOTALLY WORTH IT!

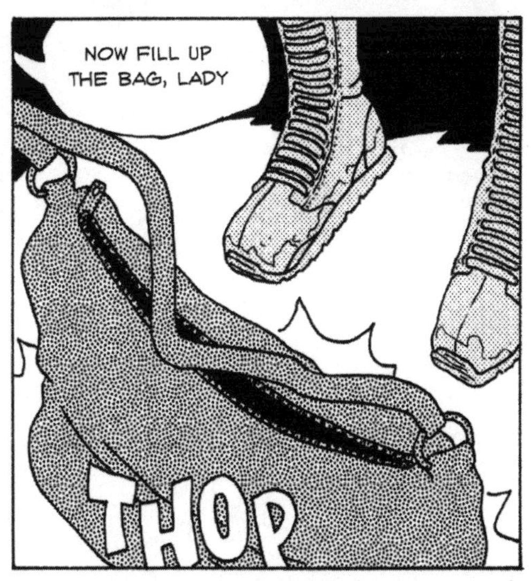
NOW FILL UP THE BAG, LADY
THOP

CALLING ME A 'BAG LADY' GRUMBLE GRUMBLE WHY I OUGHTA

HEY WHY ARE THERE THREE OF YOU NOW?

WHAT THE HECK ARE YOU ON ABOUT, THERE AIN'T THREE OF
OOOOH MY GUUAAAHH
CHOMP

BOOM
DAG BLASTED VARMINT
JOG ON

YOU OKAY, BUD?
GLLKLLKK
...GUESS NOT

WELP, A BIGGER SHARE OF THE LOOT FOR ME, RIGHT TOOTS?
TOOTS?
?

WHERE'D SHE GIT TO?

OH YEAH FORGOT THAT HAPPENED

GOOD THING I GOT THIS
BOOP

BOING

TIME TO GET OUTTA DODGE BEFORE THE POOP HITS THE FAN. MAYBE PICK UP A TUNA SUB ON THE WAY HOME?

WHERE'D YOU THINK YER GOIN', MISSY?
I THINK I'LL BE TAKIN' THAT SWEET, SWEET RIDE, TOO

OH, UH, I DON'T THINK YOU'LL BE NEEDING IT SOON

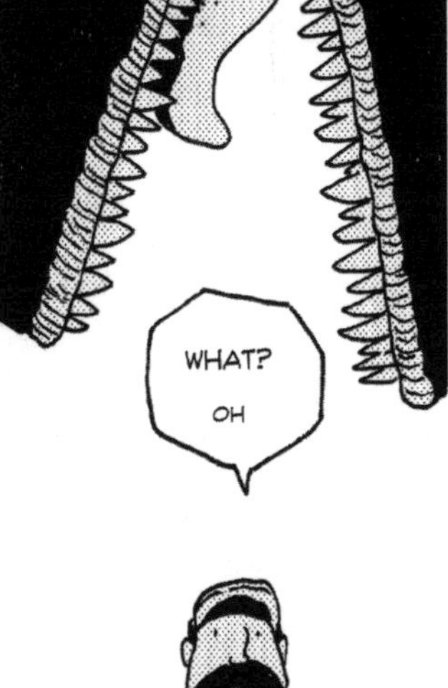
WHAT?
OH

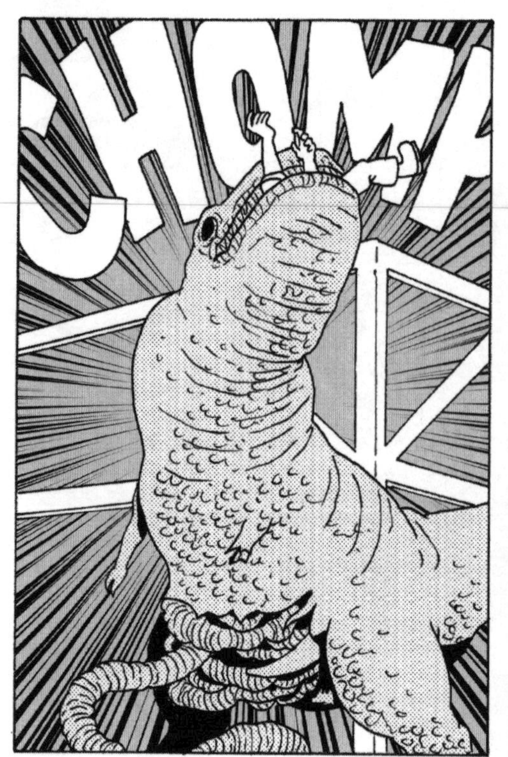
CHOMP

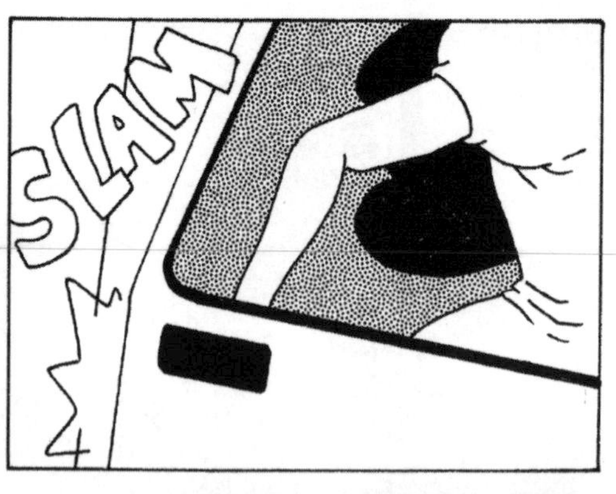
SLAM

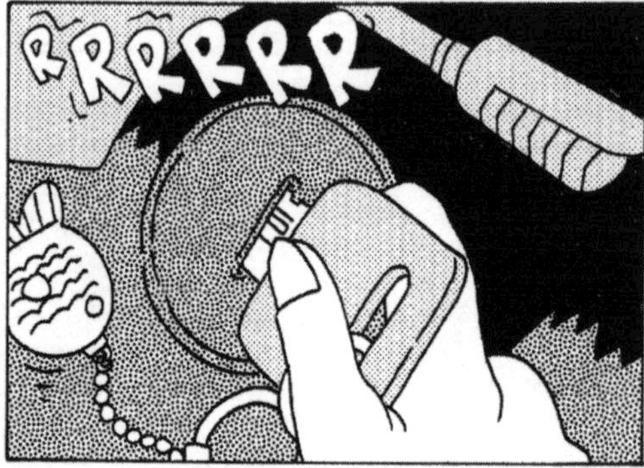
RRRRRR

RRR?
TOOT TOOT
C'MON DORIS, LET'S GO FIND US SOME MORE MISCHIEF
UARRR
THAT'S THE SPIRIT. TALLY HO!
END

ULY.
THE LAST I SAW OF MY GIRLFRIEND, STRANDS OF HER WERE CAUGHT IN HER BEST FRIEND'S TEETH.

Em... Emma...?

Emma!

Oh shit, oh **shit.**
Oh, fuck **me**, oh shit.

I WAS LUCKY - EVERYTHING I'D NEED TO SURVIVE WAS ALREADY PACKED IN THE CAR FROM MY BUSINESS TRIP.

QUARANTINE ZONE ONE
ALL EXIT AND ENTRANCE IS PROHIBITED BY LAW

ANOTHER FEW HOURS AND I'D NEVER HAVE BEEN ABLE TO LEAVE THE CITY AT ALL.
THEY DON'T KNOW WHAT IT IS, OR HOW IT'S TRANSMITTED. YOU CAN'T TELL WHO'S INFECTED UNTIL THEY'RE DEAD.

CITIES ARE BURNING, THE COUNTRY UNDER QUARANTINE. NON-EMERGENCY TRAVEL IS RESTRICTED.
COMMUNICATIONS ARE ERRATIC. INFORMATION IS SCARCE AND UNRELIABLE.

THEY TELL ME I WAS LUCKY.

THE END OF THE PIER SHOW
BY ANDREW CHEVERTON

IT'S BEEN OVER A WEEK NOW. I THOUGHT THE FAMILY WOULD COME HERE, IF THEY COULD.

Mr Punch, **where** is the **baby?**

WE USED TO HOLIDAY HERE EVERY YEAR WHEN WE WERE KIDS.
OUR HOME AWAY FROM HOME – NOW IT'S JUST ANOTHER GHOST TOWN.

He was **such** a noisy baby.
BUT WITH NO MEANS OF COMMUNICATION, I COULDN'T THINK OF WHERE ELSE TO GO.
B&B
What's **happened** to the baby?

I DON'T THINK ANYONE I KNOW IS STILL ALIVE.

He went walky, walky, walky and fell out of the **window.**

THEY'RE SOMEWHERE IN THE CITIES, SHOULDER TO SHOULDER WITH ALL THE OTHER LOST LOVED ONES.

ROWS OF CONCRETE BUILDINGS, UNMARKED MONUMENTS TO ALL THE NEW DEAD.

AUGUST.
SIX WEEKS, AND STILL NO WORD. THE SYSTEM IS COLLAPSING AND I'M STILL BESIDE THE SEASIDE, BESIDE THE SEA.

"What – three times over?"
"Not three times over, only once will be enough–
"–Mr Punch, you are going to suffer."
WHEN SHE WAS SMALL, MY LITTLE SISTER ALICE COULDN'T PRONOUNCE PUNCH AND JUDY.
WE'VE CALLED IT 'PUNGENT DOODY' EVER SINCE.

IT'S THE ONLY CONSTANT I HAVE LEFT HERE – THE ONLY TIE I FEEL TO THE PAST, TO THE WORLD OF FRESH HOT PIZZA, QUIZ SHOWS, AND EVERYTHING WE TAKE FOR GRANTED.

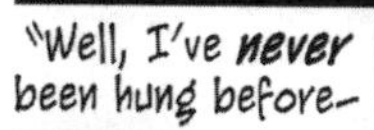
"Well, I've never been hung before–

"–Perhaps you could show me how to do it?"

I WATCH THE SHOW BECAUSE IT REMINDS ME OF ALICE AND THE HOLIDAYS WE ALL USED TO SPEND HERE YEARS AGO.
IT'S ALL I HAVE LEFT OF A WORLD WHICH NO LONGER EXISTS.

"Show you 'ow to do it?–
"–Shall I show 'im 'ow to do it?–

"–I s'pose I'd better, else we'll be 'ere all day–
"–You walks right up to the gallows like this–
"–You says all your sorries and then you puts your old head in the noose like this."

SOMETIMES THERE'S A SMALL CROWD. MOST OF THE TIME – LIKE TODAY – I'M ALONE.

SO I WATCH THE PUNGENT DOODY BY MYSELF, AND AFTERWARDS I CHECK THE TENT.

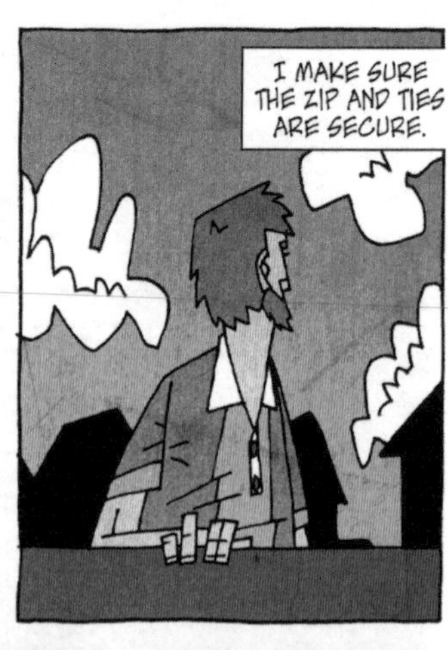
I MAKE SURE THE ZIP AND TIES ARE SECURE.

AND I WONDER JUST HOW LONG THE PUNCH AND JUDY MAN HAS BEEN DEAD.

That's the *way* to do it!
Rooty **Tooty** Tooit!

AND WHEN HE CAME BACK.

I WONDER THAT HE HAD NOBODY ELSE TO NOTICE.

FAR OUT TO SEA, I WATCH A GULL PLUCK A FISH FROM THE WATER.
A BRIEF FLASH OF LIGHT REFLECTED OFF SCALES AND DROPLETS.

I WATCH FOR A LONG TIME BEFORE HEADING BACK.

THE END

...AND FINALLY, MEMBERS OF PROTEST GROUP AND STREET MOVEMENT HELD A DEMO IN UGLYTOWN SQUARE TODAY, PROTESTING AGAINST WHAT THEY CALL 'PREFERENTIAL TREATMENT FOR THE LIVING'...
WHAT DO WE WANT!
BRAINS!
MULTIVULTURAL BRITAIN
WHEN DO WE WANT IT!
BRAINS!
BBC
NEWS 24
14:23
ZOMBIE DEMOS POORLY (ORGAN)ISED
get it?
HEADLINES
bies stupidity linked to drop in GCSE standards | police baffl
IN ADDITION, THEY DEMANDED THE RIGHTS TO PROTECT THEIR TRADITIONAL CULTURE OF EATING HUMAN FLESH, WALKING SLOWLY AND MUMBLING. THERE WERE TWO ARRESTS, ONE FOR DRUNKEN BEHAVIOUR, THE OTHER FOR LITTERING.

POLICE ESTIMATE ONLY THIRTY PEOPLE ATTENDED THE DEMO.
THIRTY, MY ARSE. THERE WERE AT LEAST ELEVENTY OF US.
IT'S A MEEJIA CONSPIRACY.
AN' I WASN'T LITTERING! IT'S NOT MY FAULT MY ARM FELL OFF WHEN I TRIED TO PUNCH THAT BREATHER.
BRAINS!
I CAN'T BELIEVE YOU DIDN'T SHARE YOUR BEER.
RIGHT! THE GLOVES ARE OFF! WE'RE GOING TO HOLD A ROOFTOP PROTEST!!!

BEATRIX POTTER ABATTOIR
THIS'LL MAKE OUR POINT. WE'RE SICK OF EATING ANIMAL BRAINS WHEN IT IS OUR RIGHT AS ENGLISH ZOMBIES TO EAT GOOD HUMAN BRAINS. WE SHALL TAKE OVER THE MEANS OF PRODUCTION!
DERE'S NOBODY ERE!
THERE'S NOBODY HERE
THERE'S NOBODY HERE
THERE'S...

ALRIGHT!
ALRIGHT!
I KNOW! THERE'S NOBODY HERE!
ACTUALLY I WAS GOING TO SAY...

THERE'S A WINDOW OPEN OVER HERE

CAREFUL! YOU'LL WRECK THE BANNER.
YOU DID PUT THE BANNER IN THERE, RIGHT DEDDYMAN?
SORT OF.

CAREFUL! I JUST GOT THAT STITCHED ON!
WHY DIDN'T YOU JUST PUT THE BANNER DOWN BEFORE YOU TRIED TO GET THROUGH THE WINDOW?
MEAT

OI! HOW DID YOU GET IN?
DOOR WAS OPEN
ISNT THE ROOF OUTSIDE BY THE WAY?

WHAT THE
I WAS WONDERING IF YOU'D NOTICE....
DEDDYMAN!

WHAT?
WHAT?

WHAT DID YOU BRING THAT FOR? NOT LIVINGIST, NOT VIOLENT, REMEMBER! THE ZDL MOTTO!

IT AIN'T LOADED!
EY! GET ORF ME!

BANG
CHNK

NOW LOOK WHAT YOU'VE DONE.
SNAP
I KNEW WE SHOULDN'T HAVE TRIED THIS SOBER.
GLUG
GLUG
OY! SAVE ME SOME.
YOU GOT A LIGHT, ANGEL?
YEAH SURE
SNKIT
SNKIT
NO!!!
SNKIT
SNKIT

BADOOOMM

LOOK OUT FOR THAT STRANGELY STILL-OPERATIVE BACON SLICER, GANGRENA!!!

AAAHHHHHHHH

CLK

ZEDDLERS
STORY BY SI SPENCER
ART BY ASH FIELDER
EDITS BY WILL VIGAR
WHAT DO WE WANT?
WHEN DO WE WANT IT?
THIS SLIGHT AND SILLY COMIC STRIP BEARS NO RELATION WHATSOEVER TO ANY TRULY HEROIC ENGLISH PATRIOTS DEFENDING THIS COUNTRY BY GETTING PISSED AND FIGHTING EACH OTHER IN CAR PARKS ACROSS THE LAND AT THE BEHEST OF A TINY CRIMINAL.

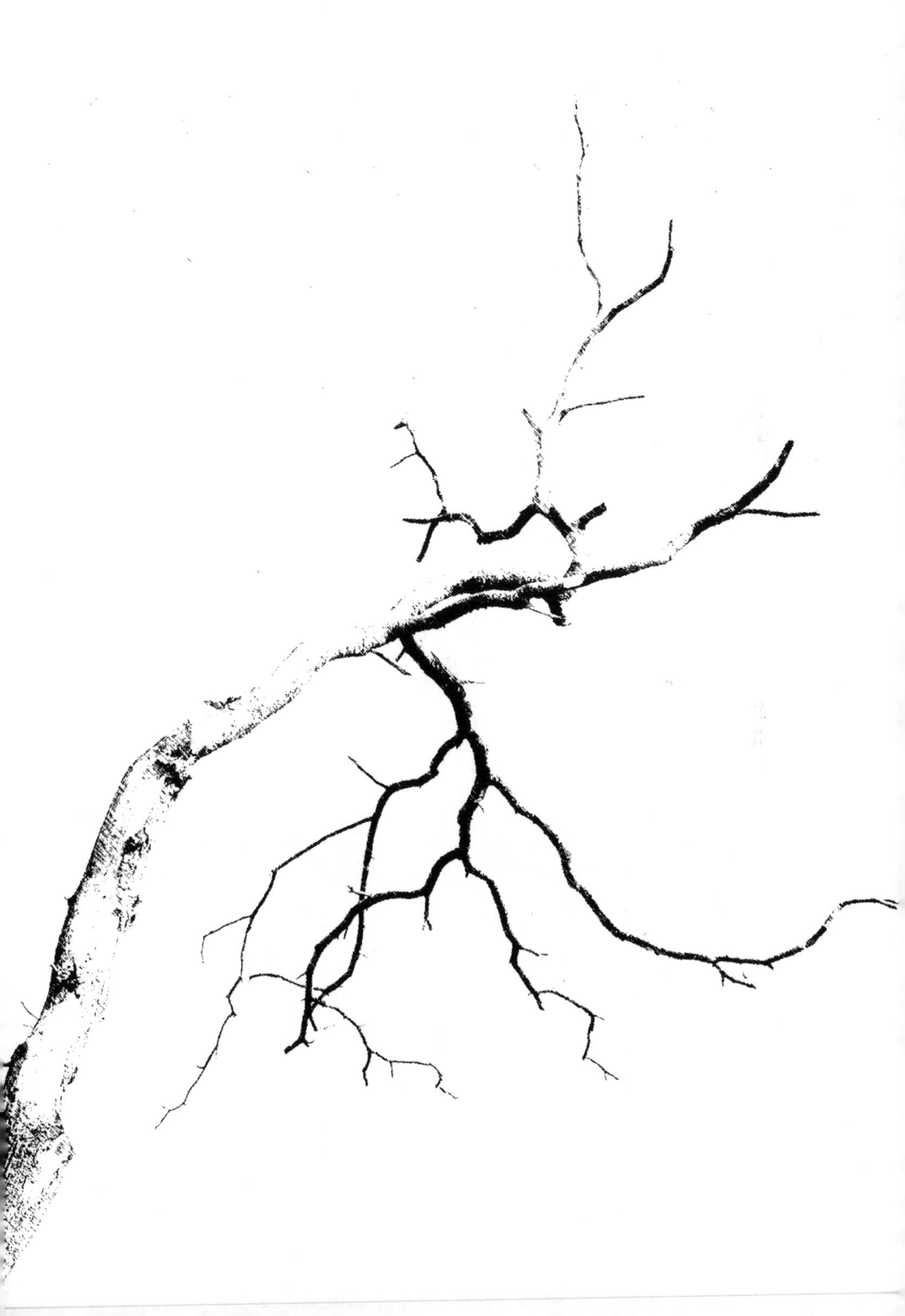

HORROR! AS YOU'VE NEVER EXPERIENCED IT BEFORE!
DICK STEIN
PAUL B. RAINEY

BUS STOP

GOOD DAY TO YOU, YOUNG MAN. YOU LOOK LIKE A MAN OF THE WORLD. LET ME INTRODUCE MYSELF...

I... AM DICK STEIN!!!

AND YOU ARE?
UM... JAKE. ALTHOUGH I AM NOT INTERESTED IN BUYING ANYTHING! I'M JUST WAITING FOR THE BUS!
AND I'M NOT SELLING ANYTHING.

YOU MAY HAVE NOTICED THAT I AM NOT LIKE OTHER MEN. THIS IS BECAUSE I AM AN ASSEMBLAGE OF BODY PARTS TAKEN FROM SOME OF BRITAIN'S MOST TALENTED ENTERTAINERS!

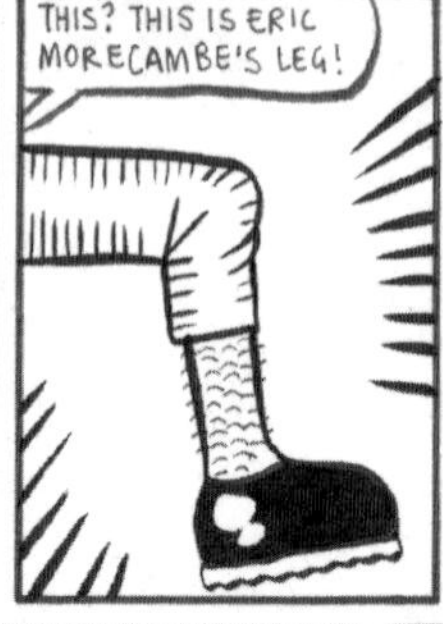
THIS? THIS IS ERIC MORECAMBE'S LEG!

AND THIS? THIS IS ROY CASTLE'S SHOULDER!

AND THIS HAND ONCE BELONGED TO PETER KAY!
BUT PETER KAY ISN'T DEAD!
NO, BUT WHEN WAS THE LAST TIME YOU SAW HIS LEFT HAND? HMM?

HMM?

AS A RESULT OF THIS COMBINATION, I AM THE GREATEST ALL-ROUND ENTERTAINER THE WORLD HAS EVER SEEN!

REALLY? CAN YOU SING?
A BIT.
CAN YOU DANCE?
A LITTLE. JUST EXISTING IS MY GIFT TO THE WORLD!

THAT AND MY GENERAL COMEDY STYLINGS.
YOU HAVE COMEDY STYLINGS?
YES, I HAVE COMEDY STYLINGS.

AND YET, DESPITE ALL THE ADVANTAGES THAT MY UNIQUE PHYSICALITY AFFORDS ME, THERE IS ONE AREA OF MY ANATOMY THAT CAUSES ME GREAT ANXIETY.

IT'S A PART OF THE BODY THAT CAUSES MOST MEN TO WORRY AT SOME POINT IN THEIR LIVES.
I DON'T LIKE THE WAY THIS IS GOING...

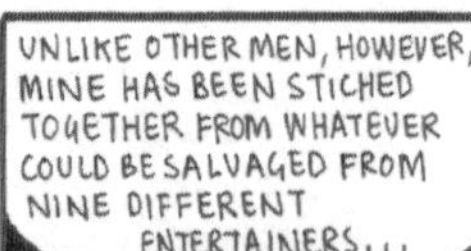
UNLIKE OTHER MEN, HOWEVER, MINE HAS BEEN STICHED TOGETHER FROM WHATEVER COULD BE SALVAGED FROM NINE DIFFERENT ENTERTAINERS...

...INCLUDING THE EXCESS ALED JONES HAD SURGICALLY REMOVED WHEN HE WAS TWELVE.
LOOK, I THINK YOU SHOULD BE TALKING TO YOUR DOCTOR...

I JUST NEED YOU TO TAKE A LOOK AT IT. TAKE A LOOK AND TELL ME IF IT LOOKS ALL RIGHT.
NO.

NO!

NOOOOOO!!!
SNIFF

belonging

words and
pictures by
kim winter

This is what
is left of the place
I grew up in

Actually, it didn't get off too
badly, but it's still a shit hole.

I was a pug ugly kid and over there
is the school where I was bullied
to the point of suicide.

I'm not that great looking now.
I didn't 'bloom'. My puppy fat
turned into dog fat.

A "double bagger", I'm afraid.

I went to university just
down the hill from here.

Even that's just rubble now

The only time I spoke
to anyone was in class

Even then you could feel the revulsion
at having to engage with me

Most of the students
spent spring and summer lounging
around on the beach
doing the things teenagers do

If ever I went there, they'd stop talking,
cover up, look the other way

It's a no-go area now, of course.
sometimes they hide in the sea
and catch you unawares

I suppose for me, it was always a no-go area.

I don't really
know why. I mean, I know
I'm not the best-looking
person in the world . . .

. . . but I'm a nice guy.
I'd look out for my friends
if I had any.

Work was no better.
I was only given an office so people
wouldn't have to look at me

This whole zombie thing made no real difference to me.

I didn't know anyone. I lived alone

When the zombies came, I was still on my own.

There were just fewer people around to hate me.

I went to live in a compound in the country. Same old same old.

I got fed up of being ignored or ridiculed, so I came home.

I have this plan, see.

Look, I'm nearly 40, still a virgin and totally alone.

Is it wrong to want to belong?

fin

29
09
13

Zombre Contributors

Tom Box

Box has inhabited Earth for 26 years and, though it is undoubtedly his least favourite planet, he remains here to share his incomprehensible mind with its inhabitants in hopes that, one day, global dominion will be his. Box exists to create. It is and always has been his one purpose. While Box does spend his entire life bringing otherworldly horrors into the human light spectrum, his talents are also available for commercial purposes, and his incredible mind has been used to achieve countless great deeds throughout the history of humanity.

Mal Earl

Mal has contributed many short stories for small press anthologies, as well as self publishing his own stand alone and serial books. Concentrating more on his own 'pulp' magazine themed Bulletproof Nylon project since 2010, he was coerced into returning to Comic production after attending the Carlisle Megacon in 2012. Interested in all aspects of Comics history and production, his goal is to produce a graphic novel totally absent of any external reference; a pure creative project – reliant solely on itself.

James Firkins

James is perhaps better known by his artistic exploits as Will Work for Whisky (aka Sunny Jim). An avid fan of graphic novels, manga, graffiti and tattoo inspired artwork, he aims to create as much as possible and claims he contributes to the world. Legend has it he is due to release a range of owls into space. He is very fond of dogs. But not too fond of dogs.

Richard Worth

Richard is one half of the Eagle Award Nominees The Water Closet. A graduate of the University of Leeds, Richard spends most of his time obsessing over the Teenage Mutant Ninja Turtles. You can read a bunch of his short stories and his on going title Ladies and Gentlemen over at www.thewaterclosetpress.blogspot.com.

Jay Eales

Jay has written, edited, published and taught comics, prose and journalism for more than a decade. Publisher of The Girly Comic and Violent!, nominated for the National Comics Awards and Comic Creators Guild Awards. The Girly Comic was twice shortlisted for a British Fantasy Award. Jay was News Features Editor for Borderline: The Comics Magazine, and has written comics for Negative Burn, The Mammoth Book of Best New Manga and Accent UK's Robots and Predators anthologies. His short stories have appeared in lots of places. He's edited loads including most recently for Obverse Books. Between 2006 and 2011, he co-organised the Caption comic convention. Find him online at: www.factorfictionpress.co.uk

Krzysztof Ostrowski

Krzysztof become known in Poland as the author of surrealistic comics including Miss Hofmokl's Shoe, based on the script by Dennis Wojda. In 2001, he formed a rock'n'roll band called Cool Kids of Death, who released 5 albums. In 2006 they played as a support for legendary Iggy Pop and the Stooges at their anniversary gig in London Astoria. Krzysztof

is currently working as a lecturer at the Academy of Fine Arts in Lodz. As well as Miss Hofmokl's Shoe, has published Plaselina, Plastelina 2 and Nowa Plastelina. His short stories have been published in numerous comic anthologies such as 44, Chopin New Romantic, and the Polish-Israeli anthology Kompot - all published by the Museum of Warsaw Uprising.

Kel Winser

Kel is the artist/writer behind the self-published comic series Just a SideKick, and the illustrator for the online comic series The Gee Bees (thegeebeescomic.co.uk). Kel lives in the flat lands of rural East Anglia. He has lots of hobbies that constantly distract him from working on his comics. This does not include his wife of whom he loves and adores and spends a proportional amount of time with outside his hobbies.

Dennis Wojda

Dennis was born in Stockholm. He lives in Warsaw where he works as a magazine designer. Dennis makes a great pesto and chocolate cake; rides a kick scooter and dreams of becoming a children's book illustrator one day. Borderline Press recently published his graphic novel 566 Frames. (www.dennissimo.com)

Joanna Sanecka

Joanna works as an editor for a website dedicated to nature in cities. She also writes articles for magazines and scripts for comics. She is the mother of two naughty boys. She loves the Baltic Sea, The Cure and watching the Moon.

Nick O'Gorman

Nick is from the west coast of Canada, and now lives in the nation's capital. He's read and collected comics as long as he can remember and has worked in the field in a variety of positions for two years. When he's not slaving over pages at his desk, Nick OG can be found playing guitar and singing in the hard rock band Sweet Alps, sampling beers and taking it easy.

Nathan Castle

Nathan was raised by sightless, translucent terrapins in the perpetual darkness of famed puppeteer Bob Carolgees's basement. Upon reaching sexual maturity he was released into the wild where he created the comic Seamonster which was read by eight people from the Internet, but a large percentage of those eight people were impressed and continued to harrass Castle for a sequel.

David Metcalfe-Carr

Dave has had a shady past in small press and indie comics. In the 90s he produced Slices, My Life Story, Modern Life Is Rubbish and Rough Trade as well as drawing two unfinished series for Rol Hirst - My Legendary Girlfriend and Escape Committee. Nowadays he spends more time as a letterer and designer, but is planning several books including reimagining Samson and Delila in the style of Get Carter. They will probably end up unfinished.

Jamie Lewis

Jamie was infected with whimsy at an early age and uses his related abilities to create unusual comics about crows that play jazz and light bulbs that ponder the purpose of existence. 'Zombeasts' is his first professional work following earlier self-published comics Justice Badger and Imaginary Stories. His most recent work in progress, Ghost Foetus is a story about the problems inherent in having your ghostly foetal twin attached to you at all times. You can read it and other oddities at freeformjazzdetectivecomics.blogspot.co.uk.

Matthew Smyth

Matthew is a writer/artist from Belfast, Northern Ireland.

Adam Steel

Artist, game designer, nerd, and zombie afficianado, Adam has been publisher and designer for DarkmooK Paper Miniatures since 2008. He enjoys good food, fine wines and long walks on the beach... but mainly his life revolves around zombies...

Gord Drynan

Gord is a Canadian writer. Nazi Zombies on Mars is his first published comic. Borderline Press may regret unleashing his outlandish imagination upon the world. Like most Canadians, Gord likes seals and other sea mammals.

Phil Buckenham

Phil lives with his lovely partner Charlotte and their family consists of their amazing son Noah and two cats Cleo and Figaro. He graduated from KIAD in 2004 with a BA in illustration and has been working as a freelance illustrator ever since. His work features action, adventure, horror, Sci-Fi, a bit of the supernatural and essentially something for everyone. Phil Buckenham's first comic series, Rented To The Dead was released in September 2013.

Peet Clack

Peet has produced work for the British small press comics scene since the late 1990s. He has contributed to anthologies such as The Girly Comic, Violent! amongst others, as well as producing his own eccentric comedy comics, Trouser Madness and Handy and Hoofy Home Hints from Afro Horse.

Baden James Mellonie

Mel is the co-creator of Edge of Extinction, with Paul Peart-Smith (2000AD) (www.edgeofextinction.co.uk) and is currently working on the Trojan series, Trojan Cry 0 and Trojan Alpha for Reaper comics (www.reapercomics.co.uk). The third graphic novel in the series Trojan Alpha: Hunted will be out in 2014. He has recently written the official N.I.C.E 2013 comic strip competition, in association with Bedford Library. Mel is also working on the horror novel End of Term and some, as yet secret projects.

Richard Whitaker

Richard is a comic artist and illustrator living in bristol. He's also a gardener and has a lovely dog called Fox.

Nigel Lowrey

Nigel was a prolific artist in the 1990s for small press titles such as The Jock and his own creation Silver. He was a contributor for Comics International, Borderline and Back Issue, has written a book on comic-based film and TV and continues to contribute to small press comics, all the while screaming at his bill-paying job for keeping him from the drawing board...

Milõs Kûntz

Milõs was born in Budapest, Hungary, he studied at the Institute of Arts in Reykjavik, before moving to Versailles.

Mitz

Mitz doesn't really like zombies but he does love dinosaurs and monster trucks so he said yes to doing a strip. He lives in Leicester with a lady who makes latex and they both want ferrets, someday.

Andrew Cheverton

Andrew is the writer of West (drawn by Tim Keable) and The Whale House (drawn by Chris Doherty), and is a contributing artist to Rol Hirst's Too Much Sex and Violence. He is currently working on his latest project, White Flesh, a body-horror giallo comic. He also keeps ants in an ant farm but argues with people who think he might like heavy metal music or emos.

Paul Rainey

Paul is a writer/artist from Milton Keynes, England. He has written and drawn some of Britain's best loved comic strips. Paul has worked for Viz magazine; worked for most of the major companies and has been part of the UK's small press contingency for many years. He has created such memorable comics as Memory Man, The Book of Lists, Thunder Brother: Soap Division and continues to plough his furrow in the comics world.

Si Spencer

Si makes up grubby stories for grubby people, sometimes in picture books, sometimes on the tellybox. Some of his grubby stories are The Books of Magick: Life During Wartime, Vinyl Underground & Hellblazer: City of Demons. He is currently working on a massively grubby story due in the more sordid stores in late 2014.

Ash Fielder

Ash is an illustrator, digital designer and comic book artist. At a young age Ash was determined to be an animator, influenced by cartoons such as Transformers, Ren and Stimpy and Hayao Miyazaki Films. After graduating in Animation in 2009 Ash Became a Freelance artist and during his time at university discovered the comic medium. Since then Ash's work is focused towards the comic medium and development work.

Kim Winter

Kim is possibly the most miserable man on the planet. Saddled with a girl's name, he has struggled to work up any enthusiasm about anything for fear that people might ask him his name. Kim believes he has written many comics, short stories and novels. That none of them have been published is probably down to inertia and an irrational fear of missing Bargain Hunt. Belonging isn't autobiographical, but might as well be.

Editor Will Vigar has been involved in the creative industries since 1980. His career as an actor came to a crashing halt when he realized he loathed musical theatre, so he become a radio and print journalist, which he did for 10 years. He has dabbled with self-publishing and small press comics, producing two volumes of Miserable, and more recently with The Slightly Odd Adventures of Alberto & Jeff. He is now with Borderline Press. He lives with his partner of 17 years and dreams of retiring to a shack in the wilds of arctic Norway.

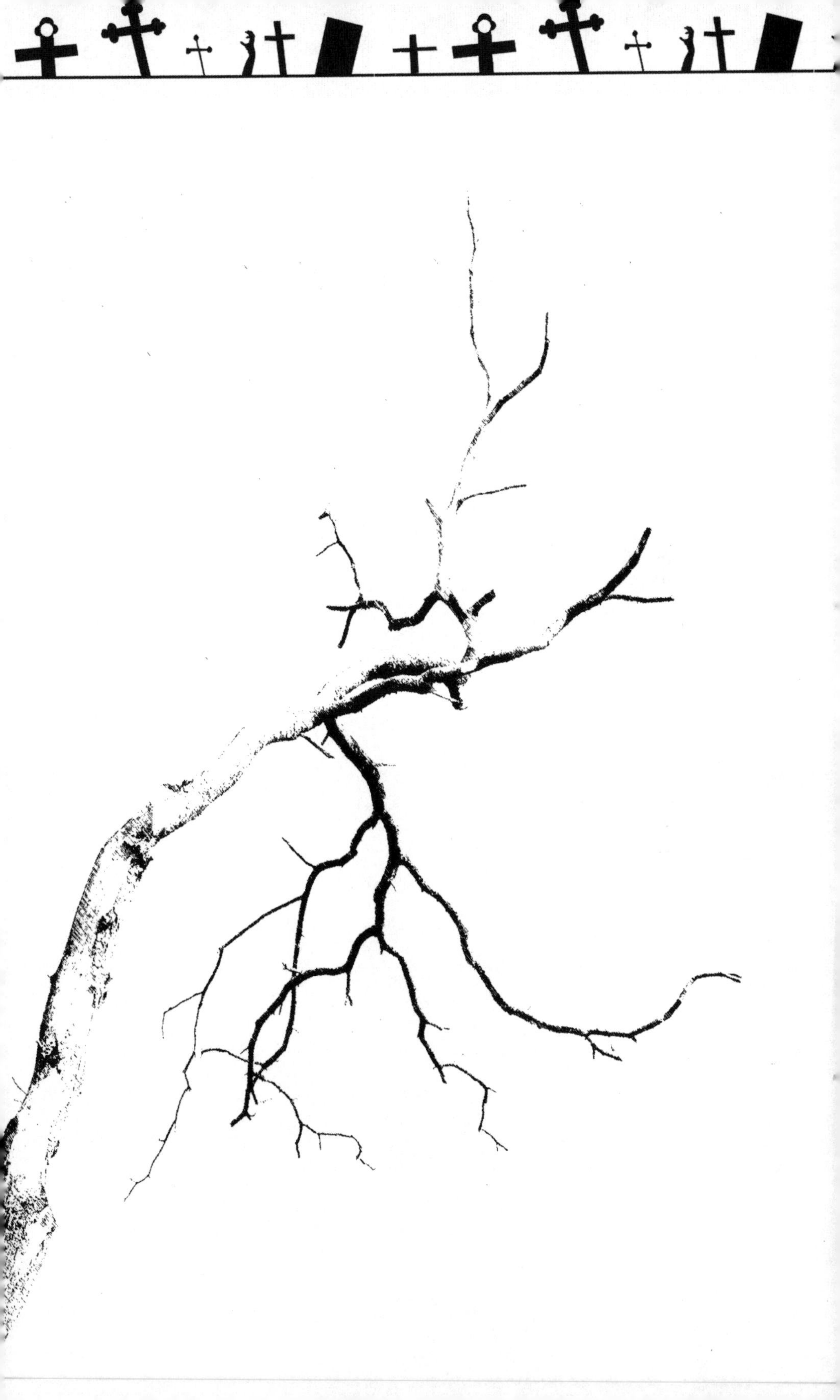